F.A.T.T. & Happy is a prized gem! Throughout th[e]
poetic and compelling style shines through as she
to embrace, celebrate, and honor our whole selves. The words come alive and
allow you to experience elevation, empowerment and positive change. You are
invited to engage with the concepts and exercises that are cleverly packaged into
this user-friendly literary tool. This is a go-to guide for embracing, loving, and
caring for all of YOU. I highly recommend you invest the time to travel this
journey of personal coaching.

Dr. Colleen Hawthorne, Concierge Psychiatric Medical Doctor & Vibrant Life Success Coach

Thoughts from Chatone's Social Media Community

"You have helped me work on loving myself, even on the outside. Your message reminds me that I have so many blessings to consider. Thank you, Chatone for sharing your encouraging spirit."

"You are such an inspiration to me!"

"You have helped me work on loving myself, even on the outside. Your message reminds me that I have so many blessings to consider. Thank you, Chatone for sharing your encouraging spirit."

"You are so passionate about what you do. Thank you for showing up with your gifts."

"You cannot know how much you inspire me."

"You remind me to celebrate all things big and small, perfect and imperfect."

"This is of great value. The keys and principles are laid out in a way completely simple to understand and apply."

"I thought I was reading a coaching book, but then it became a journal that made me examine myself physically and emotionally. Well done!"

F.A.T.T.

&

Happy

A 25 Week Plan To
Focus Attention & Take Time
While Embracing Your Waist
And Discovering Joy

Chatone Babette Morrison

This book is dedicated to
all the women who have decided
that living stuck in the
city of 'not good enough'
is no longer enough.

&

To my Dad, Linwood Curley, Jr.
who told me:

"Never Stop Writing!"

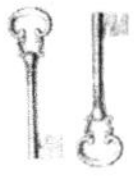

KEYS

WEEKLY KEYS

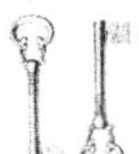

Acknowledgements

This book comes after many years of sitting on my laptop and dancing around in my brain and alternately, in pieces, on various blogs, Facebook groups, social media posts, in my coaching practices and in my conversations. I'm so grateful that it is finally on paper!

My happiness isn't possible without my Creator, Jehovah God. Almost every day I see something that He created that puts a smile on my face and helps me put aside the annoyances. I am always looking, so I am blessed to witness beauty in nature every single day. In Gratitude - I Focus Attention. I Take Time.

I'm thankful for you, Mom, for giving me such good genes and for nurturing all sorts of creativity in us. From the time I could hold a pen, I told you I was a writer. Thank you for believing it. When I stuffed letters and poems under the bathroom door, thank you for reading them. Making you proud and having your love means more than you know.

Thank you to Eva, my mother-in-love, for being my friend. The meals you made the last month I was preparing this book was just what I needed. Your support is immeasurable, and I'm so glad I've had a chance to share life with you all these years. I love you, Honey!

Thank you to Jason Winters, fellow "master-minder" and coach, younger brother and friend, for listening to me rant. I appreciate every critique and piece of "feed forward" you gave to me. Alexis and Xavier, thanks for letting me borrow your dude and your dad. You are family!

Thank you to LaTasha White, master coach and author, for cheering me on and truly being an entrepreneurial accountability partner. You rock!

Glam Guru, Daria Wright, thank you for the gorgeous branding photo and for Face-timing with me into the wee hours of the night, on our trans-state dual-creative dates. Love you, little sister.

Thank you, Dr. Kim, for encouraging a bigger vision for my "little journal". I am so glad that I, "flowed with you!"

Acknowledgements (Continued)

*FATT and Happy Life Facebook group and Instagram followers – you are wonderful!
Sharing my joyful moments make them last longer – and that is what we all need!*

*One million thanks, roses, chocolates, hugs and juicy kisses on both cheeks to my big
sissy, Cherie Arias. You let me ramble on about everything - ALWAYS. You make time for
me and every little dream I have ever had. I am so thrilled that no matter what - I get to
love you forever! You are the complete package!*

*Katelin Cherie, you are such a rare talent and a great inspiration. You are an amazing
and beautiful daughter. I'm so grateful I had you. Much of what I do is so I can show you
it's possible. And watching you navigate has taught me more than you can imagine.
Thank you for making me desire to be a better woman.*

*Levi Joseph, what would my life be without you to round out my seriousness with so much
sarcasm and laughter? You are the best tech support! Thank for wearing the first
iteration of the FATT & Happy shirt! And especially for filling my bottle with ice and
water when I'm working late. You always know when I'm thirsty!*

*To Mark Morrison, my forever boyfriend and lover for life, thank you for bringing me
home all those years ago. I'm eternally grateful that you let me be, The Princess of
Positivity™ . You are the best writing partner in the world. I never have to wonder if you
know what word I need. You have it! All I have to do is ask. Shug, you have my heart.
Always have. Always will.*

**Confidence doesn't just happen.
We are all works in progress.**

Keep Working.

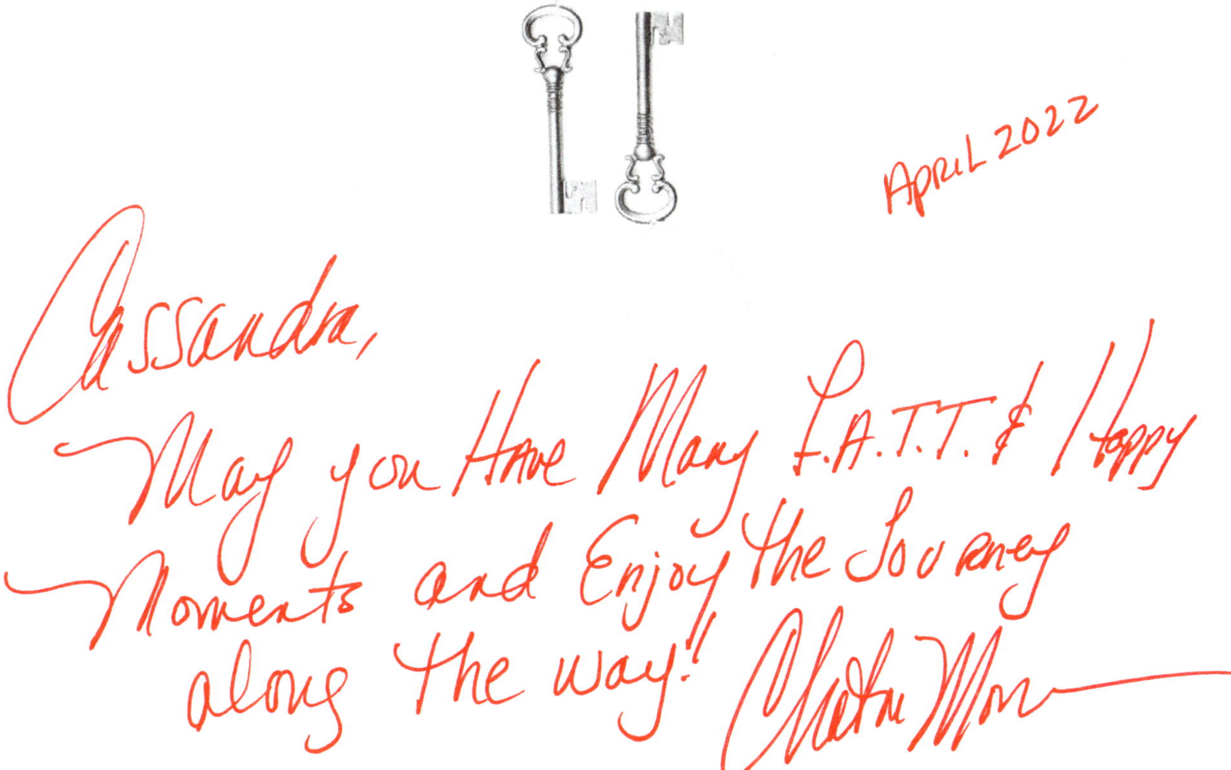

INTRODUCTION

I've been asked over and over, "Chatone, why FATT & Happy? You couldn't find any other titles? No one is fat and happy. Are they?"

The answers in order are simple:
Because I had to. Of course, I did. Yes, they absolutely are!

This is not a weight loss book. This is also not a be-as-big-as-you-want-and-binge-all-day-because-you-are-great-no-matter-what book. This is a cross-the-chasm-to-embrace-your-whole-you book. This is a discovery book. This book is a journey.

To succeed in this 25-week journey, you *will* need to change what you consume – especially in your thoughts. You will need to exercise more – especially your positive mindset. And if there is a diet in this book, the goal is to lose the heaviness of negativity and gain the light of positivity, until it reigns.

Happiness Is Elusive

Happiness can be a fleeting feeling and we learn to live without it. We get to a certain age and don't strive for it anymore. There are so many negative things headlining in our lives, that the exercise of getting to and maintaining the smallest pocket of happiness becomes a struggle. And it's not just outside elements. As women, the sword is double-edged. Stressors also come from the inside. Sometimes, *we* are the reason we can't move to a happier place. We ourselves are to blame. But you know what? Just like there are struggles inside of us – there are also solutions. We have to find a way to add yeast and watch the win rise.

Our bodies crave balance and our hormones fight to keep us in check. Although we are hard wired to deal with stress and negativity, too much makes us sick. And since we are created in such an amazing way, happy, hopeful, optimistic, and positive thoughts actually tweak the way our brains function. Every time we purposefully focus our attention on the positive, instead of the all-consuming negative, we are giving self-care to the brain.

I Promise - This Is NOT Going to Be Hard

What we are going to do together is neither complicated nor time-consuming. It's the positivity exercise that I've been doing for over 10 years. And it works. It's the law of substitution on steroids. Out with the bad, in with the good. Out with the old, in with the new. Switch that view, for this view. And on and on. Over time, this practice has changed the way I think and feel. Feeling inadequate, unattractive, fat, old, ugly or just plain "not good enough" comes and goes. Doing what I suggest in this book eases those feelings, one micro-mini block at a time. And it's called: *FATT & Happy*.

FATT and Happy is a daily discipline that takes just a few minutes. It's true, we can't control most of what happens in our daily lives. But when we spend a few minutes getting quiet, we gain some level of control. We have control over what we see, hear, smell, taste, experience and remember. When we compile these daily moments and recall them throughout the day, a "microburst" of positivity occurs. It may be small. It may be temporary. But like short lightning strikes and nearly silent thunder, the impact is profound. Change is happening.

Why You Need This

FATT and Happy was first published on my blog called *Positivitales*. I committed to record 1500 positive encounters every day for one year. I invited others to join me. I wanted to celebrate life's simplicity and find happiness in the mundane and often ignored, stuff of life. Every day I looked forward to seeing life in a new way. I was actively looking for things in which to fall in love. I was on a mission to Focus Attention & Take Time with my environment, my family, my community, my relationships, and nature. When I paid attention, I saw more things. When I was looking for things to enjoy, I stopped beating myself up for things like my belly, my thighs, my arms, and my stretch marks.

Let me ask you a question. Have you ever felt like mirrors are enemies, strategically placed in your life to make you want to stick a needle in your eye? Have you ever passed a mirror and muttered something demoralizing under your breath? When? Yesterday evening? This morning? Just now as I mentioned the word mirror? Stop. Right. Now. Focus Attention and Take Time on something that builds you. You are worth it, and it will work if you keep at it.

As women, we spend far too much time worrying about the negative, and not enough time on what is good. Despite what everyone's social media feed suggests, life is not always rich, massively successful, amazing, wonderful, beautiful or fabulous. But in every single day there is goodness. Simple goodness is simply everywhere. You don't have to wait for a special occasion once or twice a year to experience it. Do it in the next 5 minutes.

Once you start to balance your thought life, you will begin to notice other doors to confidence, and you will want to open them. How's your communication with others? What mask are you wearing? Are you plagued with energy-drainers? In between creating your own FATT & Happy list, this book provides one key topic each week for you to work through so you can begin to unlock how you really feel and execute personal success strategies.

For me, after years of living in a constant state of negative judgement centered on the imperfect composition of my body, and its inability to be instantly controlled, I found a way to simple self-acceptance. I didn't feel like I was letting myself down or like I was giving up on myself. I just felt a level of acceptance, and with it, a level of peace.

Getting Started

As a coach, I have used the Keys in **FATT & Happy** to help many women to move a "new state of mind". When you release negativity, you allow positivity to reign. When positivity reigns, you are not bogged down with the size of your waist. Or the "experience" lines on your face. Or the tiny flaws that are the complete package of you.

Focus Attention. Take Time. Enjoy your uniquely, beautiful life.

This is not my most flattering photo. I'm not made up or filtered and my hair is in its work-at-home mom state. It's here because I was so happy. This is the first day I wore the "FATT" branded t-shirt. I was traveling and people kept staring while I was in the airport. Most gave a funny kind of look, then smiled. Others looked as if they wanted to hug me. I got a few winks from older gentlemen. A few more up and down accepting nods from younger guys. All the while, I thought there was something in my teeth. It wasn't until I mentioned it to my son that I understood what was happened. He said, "Mom…it's your shirt!" I won't know for sure, but I can tell you one thing I didn't feel - self-conscious for wearing the "F" word!

Feel Good!
Chatone Morrison, 2020

Don't just sit there. Find Your Keys and Open Something!

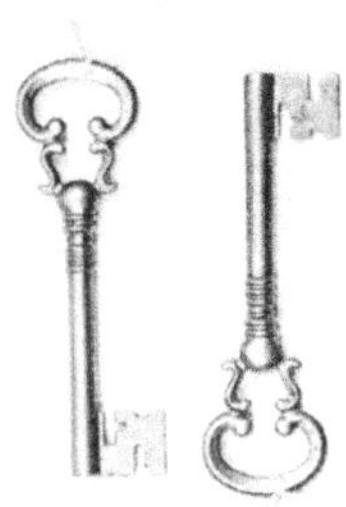

How to Use This Book

This book has been lovingly created with you in mind. It has been uniquely prepared for harmonious discovery and growth. To experience sustained changed, it is most effective to do the exercises daily. To get your thought life and mindset stronger, everyday practice is vital. For best results, you should complete one key each week. However, I designed it to allow you to start again at any time and still see your progress without negative judgement.

This journal is broken into 25 weeks or Keys and each Key is broken into the following sections:

- Discovery
- Consider
- FATT & Happy Moments
- My Key Reflections & Notes

In the **Discovery** and **Consider** sections you will find thought provoking questions and a small space to record your answers. Your first thoughts are the best thoughts. This is not the time for overthinking. If you need additional space, consider grabbing a simple journal or notebook and journaling your thoughts.

In the **FATT & Happy** section, I tease you with three things that I have enjoyed over many years of recording "micro-mini" motivational moments. Then you have three spaces to record yours. Your job is to collect three experiences and keep a record of them right here in this book. If keeping this book with you is inconvenient, by all means type or voice record them into your smart device. Before you retire for the evening, be sure to write them here. Think of this as making deposits in a positivity account. The dividends will make you wealthier each week!

A **Key Reflections & Notes** section is provided weekly. These pages are reserved for free writing, doodling, overflow, abundance, affirmations, a-ha's and discoveries, from bitter to sugary sweet. You are encouraged to be poetic, rant, rage, let it out, and let it go. At the bottom of the Key Reflections section there is a suggested intention to work on for the upcoming week. Choose to use the suggested intention or set your own. Either way, set intentions each week and work at making them a reality!

What do you need to discover, consider and reflect on the most right now? This might be the perfect place for you to start. Think about it – what would happen if regardless of your age, career path, family situation, marital status, and even where you currently fall on the scale, you blessed yourself with microbursts of honesty and joy every single day? It's time to find out. Turn the page and START!

Artistic Anchor® "Bellies Are For Embracing" Chatone Morrison ©2012
Visit chatonemorrison.com/artisticanchorsgallery, to view images in full color.

25 Keys
To
Focus Attention
&
Take Time

Key 1

APPRECIATING LITTLE THINGS

*Simplicity. Basics. The little everyday pleasures that are often overlooked. These moments are what make life great. There are many big things in your life that you cannot control. But you **can** control how you see your world. That's what FATT & Happy is all about. What will change when you Focus Attention and Take Time?*

1. **Find a quiet spot for this exercise. For a moment, sit in complete silence. Think about your friends, family, and your environment. Who or what is the one thing that you are the most grateful for at this very moment? Be specific.**

2. **What is one thing that has worked out for you despite the hardships and challenges you have experienced?**

3. **What simple things bring you joy?**

1. How often do you purposely think about or do things that bring you laughter and joy? Do you remember the last time you had a huge smile you simply couldn't control? Journal about it.

2. If you haven't purposely put joy and laughter in your life, what has prevented you from doing so? And if you have, what has been the motivation?

3. For the next 30 days, how willing are you to start looking for things that bring laughter, joy or peace into your life? Make a commitment to yourself! Be sure to record them daily in the FATT & Happy journal at the end of each "Consider" section.

FATT & HAPPY THOUGHT

Make time to find joy. It's closer than you think. LOOK.

What things will you remember each day this week? What will you see, hear, experience, feel, or do? What will bring warmth, smiles, contentment and joy? Focus Attention and Take Time!

Get FATT & Happy!

DAY 1

Knowing more than before
Slowly washing my hair
Coconut oil in my palms
Now It's Your Turn!

1.

2.

3.

DAY 2

Pine cones left behind
Giving for no special reason
Reminiscing with old friends
Now It's Your Turn!

1.

2.

3.

DAY 3

A little girl's voice wishing her daddy well
Glare of bright sun on the pavement
Feeling cold and warm at the same time
Now It's Your Turn!

1.

2.

3.

DAY 4

Knowing you can always start over
Hearing planes overhead that you cannot see
The smell of lavender
Now It's Your Turn!

1.

2.

3.

DAY 5

A clean house at the end of a long day
Making plans for a girls' night out
Mothers-in-law that treat you like their own
Now It's Your Turn!

1.

2.

3.

DAY 6

Looking at the sky through paper snowflakes
Hot pink permanent markers
Meeting a Deaf stranger and spelling your name in ASL
Now It's Your Turn!

1.

2.

3.

DAY 7

The aroma of fresh bread baking
Being able to move on when it's time
Detached compassion
Now It's Your Turn!

1.

2.

3.

I will focus, pay attention, and take the time to embrace joy in little things for at least 5 minutes each day this week.

Key 2

AND YOUR BEST GOES TO . . .

Live Your Best Life…Best Life Ever
These have become adages we hear every single day. But, aside from you personally, how do you decide who gets your best? Every day you have the opportunity to show up in your life and give your best self or a mediocre second, or even third. It takes work, but great and honest relationships result. How often do you give your best, and to whom are you giving it? And do you remember to add yourself to the list?

1. Think for a minute about the most important people in your life. When you consider their vulnerabilities and emotional state, who is it that *absolutely needs* your love, patience, understanding and friendship right now?

2. On the other hand, who is taking your emotional energy? Do they deserve it?

3. Now that you know "who" needs you most, identify "what" they need from you. For example: Forgiveness? Attention? Affirmation? Direction? Acceptance? Or something else? Explore what it will feel like to provide that support.

1. Look back. How often do you consider who needs the best from you? Do you find that who receives your best is always the same person, without truly looking at the needs of other people? Which of your children, siblings, parents, or friends *always* gets your best, even when you are neglecting others?

2. Do you automatically give your best to this person because you feel it is what a good mother, sister, daughter, friend *should* do?

3. What happens when you recognize that a new co-worker or team member needs to hear your story of survival and success? Or, perhaps an in-law feels out of place in the family and could desperately use a friend. What could you do to provide ease for them? How willing are you to step out of your comfort zone and extend yourself to someone that may not be a VIP in your life?

FATT & HAPPY THOUGHT

There will be days that giving "half" is more powerful than giving your "all". Know the difference, do what you can, and by all means, put yourself on the list. You deserve to get the best of you too!

What things will you remember each day this week? What will you see, hear, experience, feel, or do? What will bring warmth, smiles, contentment and joy? Focus Attention and Take Time!

Get FATT & Happy!

DAY 8

10-year-olds singing on the school bus
Not needing to be right
Sharing an encouraging story with family
Now It's Your Turn!

1.

2.

3.

DAY 9

Sharing music with my kids
Having a shoulder to cry on
Dark chocolate melting in my mouth
Now It's Your Turn!

1.

2.

3.

DAY 10

Being a shoulder to cry on
Just enough toilet paper in the middle of the night
The murals at Gia's Restaurant, Little Italy, Baltimore
Now It's Your Turn!

1.

2.

3.

DAY 11

The shadow of a full tree in summer
Chocolatey babies that look like dolls
Family game night
Now It's Your Turn!

1.

2.

3.

DAY 12

Mix-matched socks on purpose
Abstract paintings on huge canvases
Tears of joy
Now It's Your Turn!

1.

2.

3.

DAY 13

Soft unexpected touches
A handful of cold cereal
Having the elevator door held for you
Now It's Your Turn!

1.

2.

3.

DAY 14

Turning your face to the sun in the middle of winter
When children discover simple
Making out with your spouse, just because
Now It's Your Turn!

1.

2.

3.

This week, I will pay attention to my self-talk and correct self-defeating language.

Key 3

ADDRESSING UNRESOLVED DECISIONS

Embracing joy everyday becomes complicated, if not, impossible when you put off making decisions. Instead of being able to move forward, you create a limbo-like environment. You can move through your day, but your stress mounts, your sleep is degraded, and you will take this out on your body or mindset in ways you had never planned. Have you been putting off a decision that you truly need to make?

1. What is the most important decision you need to make in your life right now?

2. What will be the result if you delay in making this decision - or what has been the result already?

3. How much stress are you undergoing because no decision has been made? Choose one and then explain how you feel.
    a. Minimum
    b. Moderate
    c. High
    d. Almost unbearable

1. **Deep down, do you know what decision you should make? If so, why are you holding back from resolving the situation?**

2. **If your daughter or sister had the same dilemma, what advice would you give? (This is most likely the same advice for you.)**

3. **Describe how you will feel once the situation is resolved.**

FATT & HAPPY THOUGHT

When you Focus Attention & Take Time, it provides your mind with the ease and grace to find solutions and act upon them. If your mind has regular refreshment, there is less need to overthink.

What things will you remember each day this week? What will you see, hear, experience, feel, or do? What will bring warmth, smiles, contentment and joy? Focus Attention and Take Time!

Get FATT & Happy!

DAY 15

Old Prince songs
Dancing in front of French doors
First inklings of love
Now It's Your Turn!

1.

2.

3.

DAY 16

Subway rides at sunset
The way I "mother" like no other
Cornflower blue
Now It's Your Turn!

1.

2.

3.

DAY 17

Bible reading and understanding
The smell of wood at Home Depot
White noise at night
Now It's Your Turn!

1.

2.

3.

DAY 18

Great selfie photo shoots
Chestnut riding boots
12 step programs
Now It's Your Turn!

1.

2.

3.

DAY 19

Winter days that feel like spring
The 100 trillion cells that make up my body
An impromptu party
Now It's Your Turn!

1.

2.

3.

DAY 20

Playing a new board game and listening to smooth jazz
Brick wall murals
Laughing out loud for no reason at all
Now It's Your Turn!

1.

2.

3.

DAY 21

English muffins with real butter
Finished First drafts
Oatmeal with cranberries as a snack in my favorite mug
Now It's Your Turn!

1.

2.

3.

This week, I will give myself permission to feel my feelings, instead of stuffing them down.

NOTES

Key 4

**REVEALING THE TRUTH:
HOW YOU "REALLY" FEEL ABOUT YOUR BODY**

In my earliest memories I did not like my body. I was only in kindergarten, but I already knew it was the wrong shape. It was too big and unwieldy. It was the object of jokes and remarks and what seemed like disgusting. I often felt disgusting. Before first grade, I learned to hate the body I walked around in every day. Those feelings held me back from doing many things I could have enjoyed. Much later, this "hated" body blessed me with my miracle daughter, who I almost lost to miscarriage. In a few moments of time, I knew I would change. How could I be a model for this precious girl unless I figured it out for myself? It took a lot of years to learn it wasn't my body holding me back. It was me. What about you?

1. **How often is your body on your mind? (For example, what you should/should not eat? How much you should exercise?) Pick one and explain.**
   a. **Almost never**
   b. **Often, 3-4 times per day**
   c. **Constantly, it is always on my mind**

2. **What is the area on your body you appreciate the most?   And what elements of your physical appearance do others tend to notice or compliment the most?**

3. **Is there an area on your body that you dislike and also you have the power to change?**

CONSIDER

1. **If you have the power to change an area of your body and choose not to, why not? Is it less important than you think? Or is there another reason? Explore.**

2. **If you have decided to refrain from working on the areas you dislike, how close are you to accepting who you are right now, and focusing on the areas you do appreciate? (What are those areas again?)**
   a. **I am not close at all**
   b. **I might be able to get there**
   c. **I am already over it**

I Am Not Close At All

If you are struggling with your body and body image and allowing it to steal your peace every day, it's possible that your concern and challenge is not solely body image. Know that getting to the root of your concerns may be best done with a professional. Take the time to honor yourself.

I Might Be Able To Get There

If you think you can, then you can! Little by little, focus on the things that you appreciate about yourself. Understand that you are in good company. Regardless of size, many women struggle and are at this stage of acceptance.

I Am Already Over It

Congratulations, You Are Doing Better Than Most Women.

FATT & HAPPY THOUGHT

I'd rather give a girl a girdle than tell her to, "hold herself in". One changes how she looks at her clothing – the other changes how she looks at herself.

Your daughter, your niece, your little sister – they are watching what you do. Be careful with your words. Good health, comfort (and beauty) comes in many sizes!

What things will you remember each day this week? What will you see, hear, experience, feel, or do? What will bring warmth, smiles, contentment and joy? Focus Attention and Take Time!

Get FATT & Happy!

DAY 22

Putting my kindness to work
Being alone and enjoying the quiet
Keeping my word
Now It's Your Turn!

1.

2.

3.

DAY 23

A silk ficus tree with white fairy lights
Jumping on a backyard trampoline
Happily speaking broken Spanish and being understood
Now It's Your Turn!

1.

2.

3.

DAY 24

Being proud of someone else's growth
Being stared down by a "friendly" pit bull
A freshly cleaned kitchen
Now It's Your Turn!

1.

2.

3.

DAY 25

A good memory
Thinly sliced Vidalia onions
Listening to my son read after breakfast
Now It's Your Turn!

1.

2.

3.

DAY 26

Leaving a red lipstick print behind
Green hills dotted with black cows
English Leather Cologne
Now It's Your Turn!

1.

2.

3.

DAY 27

10,000 steps by noon
Scoops of ice cream in old fashioned silver bowls
Standing amidst history at The African American Museum in DC
Now It's Your Turn!

1.

2.

3.

DAY 28

Getting "dolled up" for a special affair
Cookies cooling on racks
The Rocky Soundtrack: Rocky's Reward
Now It's Your Turn!

1.

2.

3.

This week, I will release one painful memory that no longer serves me.

Key 5

WHAT YOUR CLOTHES SAY

It's been said that clothes make the woman, but that is only a part of the story. If other people always like what you wear, but you feel self-conscious, you will suffer a negative impact. What you put on your body can make you feel accomplished and confident, or out of place and uncomfortable. The clothes you wear tell a story. The message doesn't have to be expensive or trendy or brand new. It needs to be a story you enjoy and don't mind retelling. What do your clothes say about you?

1. If you saw *yourself* casually walking in the mall every day for ten days, how many days out of ten would you like the way you are dressed? Do the same exercise for what you wear while working.

2. Describe your style. Why do you make these choices?
    a. Conservative
    b. Simple
    c. Bohemian and colorful
    d. Trendy
    e. Energetic and independent
    f. Other (fill in)

3. What do you think people would assume about your personality based on how you dress? Would they be correct?

1. Pick one choice that describes what story your style is telling. Are you happy with the choice?
   a. You are out of date and prefer to be alone
   b. Your personality is not identified solely by what you wear
   c. You are independent and choose to dress according to how you feel that day
   d. You love your curves, your muscular physique, or your petite frame, and have no reason to hide it

2. Dressing up generally elevates your credibility in the eyes of other people. Dressing casually makes you seem more approachable. What do your style choices say about you? Explain.
   a. Add credibility and respect
   b. Make people think you are shallow and rebellious
   c. Leave people confused
   d. Reveal little, and that is how I want it

3. What do you want your clothes to say about you?

FATT & HAPPY THOUGHT

Professional Stylist & Coach, Shaye Cunningham drops these gems on her clients:*
"Your closet is precious real estate. Fill it with things that honor you."
"Your body composition is not your fault. Every woman should dress the way she's been blessed."
"A confident mindset will help you shop wisely and stop wearing clothes that don't fit or flatter."
"Your clothing size is only a number. Stop wasting time on small things that do not matter."

What things will you remember each day this week? What will you see, hear, experience, feel, or do? What will bring warmth, smiles, contentment and joy? Focus Attention and Take Time!

Get FATT & Happy!

**See Additional Resources for more information about Shaye Cunningham.*

DAY 29
The first kiss of the day
Stiff grass under bare feet
Kids turning back for one last wave
Now It's Your Turn!

1.

2.

3.

DAY 30
Juicy limes
Celebrating something small
Shaking my body on the front row of Zumba class
Now It's Your Turn!

1.

2.

3.

DAY 31
Hot honey and lemon
Refinished oak dressers
Stevie Wonder's song, "Black Orchid"
Now It's Your Turn!

1.

2.

3.

DAY 32
Touching my toes first thing in the morning
Unbraiding my daughter's hair
The sweet smell of coconut oil
Now It's Your Turn!

1.

2.

3.

DAY 33

Worshipping as a family in peace
A calm heart
The right words at the right time
Now It's Your Turn!

1.

2.

3.

DAY 34

Seeing sunlight's afterglow on my eyes
Towels hot from the dryer
Eating to live and loving it
Now It's Your Turn!

1.

2.

3.

DAY 35

Dr. Teals Bath Salts
Laughter created by me
Screaming loud during a workout
Now It's Your Turn!

1.

2.

3.

Each day this week, I will give a compliment to someone I encounter.

Key 6

TAKE ACTION AGAINST ENERGY DRAINERS

Having a positive perspective is extremely powerful. But let's face it, you often must deal with energy draining people and activities that you simply cannot avoid. Have you ever experienced a gut reaction, a sudden headache, food cravings out of nowhere, etc.? If you have a stressful, negative, visceral reaction to a person or situation, consider this an energy drainer. Ignoring this or pretending it doesn't matter can influence your entire outlook. What is the source of your energy drainers?

DISCOVERY

1. **Describe who or what consistently drains your energy. What do you feel when it happens? (For example: tired, sad, hungry, depressed, etc. Do not judge it. Just acknowledge and describe. You cannot release what you refuse to acknowledge.)**

2. **When and where do you feel that your energy is consistently at its highest and lowest? Who are you with, and what are you doing? How does the way you respond to your highest and lowest energy differ?**

3. **Finish this sentence: I am allowing this energy draining person or situation to remain in my life due to…**
   a. **Habit**
   b. **Fear of letting go**
   c. **Loyalty**
   d. **Not knowing how to release**
   e. **Something else:**

How would it feel to transition away from these feelings?

CONSIDER

Sometimes we drain our own energy. For example, a very common self-inflicted energy drainer is trying to get someone to like you when they have made it clear that they do not. Another is telling your goals and aspirations to someone who is not worthy to have them or has no interest in your growth.

1. Is there anyone in your life that doesn't like or respect you, but you still find yourself over-giving and trying hard to make them accept you? Why is it so important that this person likes you? What do you fear will happen if they don't accept you? Journal and Release.

2. Create Strategies. What are your favorite energy-fueling activities? Who are your key energy-giving associates? Make a detailed list and think about how you can spend more time in those activities and with those people.

FATT & HAPPY THOUGHT

Getting the respect you want may be easier and less stressful than trying to get people to like you. Focus Attention & Take Time with Energy Givers - Not Energy Drainers!

What things will you remember each day this week? What will you see, hear, experience, feel, or do? What will bring warmth, smiles, contentment and joy? Focus Attention and Take Time!

Get FATT & Happy

DAY 36

Handwritten letters
Optimism
Knowing I have a Creator
Now It's Your Turn!

1.

2.

3.

DAY 37

Wild bamboo
Taking off the training wheels
People watching people
Now It's Your Turn!

1.

2.

3.

DAY 38

The sound of a paint roller
An ironed white shirt with the collar up 80's style
Ticking grandfather clocks
Now It's Your Turn!

1.

2.

3.

DAY 39

Photographs matted in dark red
Feeling safe enough to share a secret
A ringing phone during lonely times
Now It's Your Turn!

1.

2.

3.

DAY 40
Being called beautiful
Acknowledging joy
Pursuing the top priority
Now It's Your Turn!

1.
2.
3.

DAY 41
Wearing slipper socks to bed
Hearing my mom's voice
Finding old movie stubs and remembering who was with me
Now It's Your Turn!

1.
2.
3.

DAY 42
Packages that arrive a day early
Listening to a baby grand piano played at the mall
Whistling while I work
Now It's Your Turn!

1.
2.
3.

Discovery: This week, I will make a list of my growth and accomplishments from the last 30 days.

NOTES

Key 7

SHAKE IT UP!

Have you ever heard of 'Stucksville'? It's a place from my dad's imagination where you end up when options seem scanty. After my son was born, I was very sick, and I took a summer long trip to Stucksville.

I had a strep through my entire body. I suffered two months of fever, sore throats, laryngitis, swollen glands, and an eye surgery before I got a proper diagnosis and the right medication. Every day was the same routine of feeling stuck, sick, powerless and exhausted – all while trying to nurse a newborn and nurture a 4-year-old.

There was one powerful saving grace. Each day, no matter how bad I felt, I went for a drive. I put the kids in the back of the car and simply went looking. I don't know exactly what I was looking for, but I needed to change the scenery, discover something new, and shake things up. I couldn't change everything, but I changed what I could - one car ride at a time.

Getting to 'Stucksville' is easy. Navigating your way back home can be a challenge, but I know you can do it. Do you have little strategies to shake up your routine, so you never feel stuck for too long?

1. **What does a typical weekday (Monday-Friday) and weekend (Saturday-Sunday) look like for you? How can you add in a few things that are new and different from your regular routine?**

2. **Review what you wrote above. Circle any new things that would interrupt your routine. What is realistic for you to incorporate into your life in the next 30 days?**

3. **When is the last time you did something new or different from your regular routine? What was it, and what good came of it?**

CONSIDER

1. Being open to trying something new can make a big difference. The following is a list of ideas:
    a. Study a new language
    b. Take a group exercise class
    c. Ask a child for advice
    d. Read a book from an unfamiliar genre
    e. Drive home the scenic way from work
    f. Work on a project backwards

Pick something from the above list that resonates with you and journal about it. If nothing resonates, journal about 2-3 other things you would like to try.

2. Create a strategy to break out of your comfort zone in the next 30 days by having a vision, writing it down and making a plan. Be forward thinking and look for opportunities both big and small. Think about how you will execute before you make the final plan and get ready to take a risk. Start here and use the note pages in the back of this book if you want more room!

FATT & HAPPY THOUGHT

*Small changes in your life will grow your confidence.
Confidence will grow your life. There is no need to overthink.
Just go slowly in the direction you need to go.*

*What things will you remember each day this week? What will you
see, hear, experience, feel, or do? What will bring warmth, smiles,
contentment and joy? Focus Attention and Take Time!*

Get FATT & Happy!

DAY 43

Trees that don't fall
Healthy blood pressure
Deep breathing and counting to 5
Now It's Your Turn!

1.

2.

3.

DAY 44

Living the truth
The jelly stained face of a 3-year-old feeding herself
The moment the light bulb takes life
Now It's Your Turn!

1.

2.

3.

DAY 45

Aging gracefully
His hand on the small of my back
Rescue workers
Now It's Your Turn!

1.

2.

3.

DAY 46

Driving without destination
Never being ashamed to say: "I'm hungry"
The wingspan of vultures
Now It's Your Turn!

1.

2.

3.

DAY 47
Cerulean blue bathroom tile
Long black cowgirl skirts
Rooting for the competition
Now It's Your Turn!

1.

2.

3.

DAY 48
Bare tree branches reaching across a parking lot
Going successfully over the Falls in a Barrel
Toddlers that say, "Thank you"
Now It's Your Turn!

1.

2.

3.

DAY 49
Being on time
Living Anchored
Knowing this life is not all there is
Now It's Your Turn!

1.

2.

3.

This week, I will do something decadent for myself and my best friend.

Key 8

TAKING THE "X" OUT OF EXERCISE

*Body confidence and positive body image doesn't arrive because you gain muscle, gain weight, lose weight, have augmentation surgery, get implants, a tummy tuck, weight loss surgery, or any of the other ways that women work hard to change who they are physically. What about exercise? For many, exercise is just another item on a list of things you **have** to do, and therefore receives mixed reviews. But the thing is, movement is one of the easiest ways to become confident and feel beautiful, regardless of how well you think you move, or even your size.*

After my daughter was born, I discovered the gym. Yes, I wanted to lose weight. But more than that, I wanted to feel my whole self in my body again and challenge its boundaries. Amazingly, in the process I fell madly in love with moving, and I learned that my body was not the enemy. What about you?
Have you placed an "X" on exercise?

1. **When was the last time you purposefully went out of your way to move your body, and what did you do? (Stretch, take the stairs, park a far distance from the market, go for a short walk during your workday, take a spin class, swim laps, lift weights, etc.)**

2. **Describe your regular exercise routine.**
    a. **How satisfied are you with it? If you are looking for particular results, what are they, and is your routine working?**
    b. **If you don't have a regular exercise routine, how does your current body size play into the reason?**

3. **What are your goals as it relates to movement? Are you happy with your answer?**
    a. **I am very movement conscious and I am constantly looking for ways to move more and do better.**
    b. **I think about it, but I don't have a regular routine. I just fit it in when I can.**
    c. **I move regularly at my job, but don't have a gym membership or anything.**
    d. **Movement is not a priority for me.**

1. Are you aware that exercise directly affects not just your body, but your sleep patterns, your memory, your energy and how you deal with stress? Journal and retain what you personally know about the benefits of exercise.

2. Think About It: What is the most important area of your body you want to support with movement?

3. Staying motivated is easier when you have a friend or group to hold you accountable. (It's ok to feel overwhelmed if you are in a large group, and if so, choose a small group, or even one person.) What strategy could you implement to get started and keep going, so you can reap the benefits of exercise and movement?

FATT & HAPPY THOUGHT

Exercise is a proven mood booster, anxiety remover and depression lifter. Use it generously and with joy!

What things will you remember each day this week? What will you see, hear, experience, feel, or do? What will bring warmth, smiles, contentment and joy? Focus Attention and Take Time!

Get FATT & Happy!

DAY 50
Copper bottom pots hanging high over head
Babies in their swings, chubby feet crossed
Floss sticks with dinosaur handles
Now It's Your Turn!

1.
2.
3.

DAY 51
Listening to the wind
Moving the furniture and having a "new" room
A man bowed on one knee in public
Now It's Your Turn!

1.
2.
3.

DAY 52
Fine art graffiti on tall bridges
Winter forests dressed by the sky
Singing along to the car radio
Now It's Your Turn!

1.
2.
3.

DAY 53
Matchbox cars with flames on the side
Suggestion boxes in old restaurants
A flawless freehand cat eye
Now It's Your Turn!

1.
2.
3.

DAY 54

Remembering my dad's giggle
Eva's 7UP Cake and talking after dinner
Short even manicures
Now It's Your Turn!

1.

2.

3.

DAY 55

Kids that read real novels
Blue ink on stark white paper
Shrimp and grits at Ruby Slipper in New Orleans
Now It's Your Turn!

1.

2.

3.

DAY 56

Rocking out wide calf boots
My mom's Sunday turkey dinner with all the trimmings
When partners cut in
Now It's Your Turn!

1.

2.

3.

This week, I will increase my movement and I will admire something about my physical appearance during the process.

Key 9

BODYCON 101

A bodycon is a type of dress that is very form fitting to the body. It means body conscious. Regardless of your size, it's meant to accentuate your figure and reveal with is underneath. However, wearing a bodycon dress is not about a body shaper or waist trainer. It's about the confidence worn underneath. Keys 4 and 5 talked about your clothes and how you feel about your body. This Key is going to help you work through lingering body self-consciousness so you can rock your bodycon. Whatever story you allow your clothes to tell about you, let it be a confident one!

1. We all have little flaws. Do you inadvertently draw attention to yours by mentioning them repeatedly? How often do you put yourself down, insult yourself or parts of your body? What is the result, and why do you do it?

2. When is the last time you took a long look at yourself in the mirror? What did you see? Be raw…it's OK. If you tend to avoid mirrors, when did that start, and why?

3. What's your initial/gut reaction when you see a larger/overweight person? What's your initial/gut reaction when you see a petite/very slender person? Do either of these body types make you feel uncomfortable or negative in any way? Explain.

1. **Body Discovery (Bra and Undies Time). This week spend time getting to know your body again by looking in the mirror for 15-30 minutes, or more. *Look at everything together*. Force yourself to see what you love and also the flaws you wish you could change. Compliment yourself. Acknowledge your beauty inside and out. Write down your discoveries.**

2. **Bodycon Fix #1. The most important fix is always LOVE. Do you have a disdain for your round belly or small chest? Spend extra time this week touching the part of you that you have been conditioned to hate. Write about the experience.**

3. **Bodycon Fix #2. Make a plan to increase your body confidence. If your belly is an issue, could you purchase a support cami or body briefer? Could you do planks before bed or standing crunches while you work? If you don't like having a small chest could you get fitted for a new padded push-up bra? Could you work in some pectoral exercises with weights?**

   Write down at least one commitment you can do this week to increase your bodycon. Set an intention and then make it happen!

FATT & HAPPY THOUGHT

Brilliance. Beauty. Flaws.
You are ALL OF IT at the same time.
Remember to look at EVERYTHING TOGETHER.

What things will you remember each day this week? What will you see, hear, experience, feel, or do? What will bring warmth, smiles, contentment and joy? Focus Attention and Take Time!

Get FATT & Happy!

DAY 57

Looking through binoculars to discover something new
Salmon for breakfast
The swoosh of my winter coat as I walk
Now It's Your Turn!

1.
2.
3.

DAY 58

Seeing a silver tree through an icicle
Lemons and limes piled high on a table
The white essence of orange left behind on my hands
Now It's Your Turn!

1.
2.
3.

DAY 59

Marking measurements on the inside of the pantry
Being brave enough to get yet another MRI
Babies that sing, "Love Me Tender"
Now It's Your Turn!

1.
2.
3.

DAY 60

Scrubbing the deck until the red shows
Swallowing hard, then speaking up
Deciding to be more
Now It's Your Turn!

1.
2.
3.

DAY 61

Open house sign on the lawn
The joy on my daughter's face when she feels pretty
Hearing: "I missed you mom"
Now It's Your Turn!

1.
2.
3.

DAY 62

Battery operated vanilla scented candles
Praying on your knees as a family
Talking to the food while cooking
Now It's Your Turn!

1.
2.
3.

DAY 63

No makeup, no filter
Catching a fish for the first time
Blurring the blue country boundaries on a globe
Now It's Your Turn!

1.
2.
3.

This week, I will call or send a card to someone who needs it and tell them about their specialness.

Key 10

TAKING OFF THE MASK

Masks have their purpose. They can be worn to disguise the true self and as a protection and shield. This can be fun, as in, an 18th century ball. This can be safe, as in, protecting your lungs from toxic fumes. Or it can be dangerous, as in, hiding your true self fearing that no one will understand you. In the age of social media, it seems everyone has developed a persona to share online, at work and even with friends. Over time you can lose who you are and who you most want to be. But who you are and how you behave at home is usually your reality.

When I was 16, I first discovered that I was living with a mask. Pretending to be happy was easier than telling the truth. Unfortunately, I had spent years feigning contentment and "playing off" a profound sadness. At 16, I found a friend who helped me take it off. She helped me to begin. I am forever grateful that she cared enough to see something, say something and do something. What about you? Are you wearing a mask?

1. How would you best describe yourself *really?* And how happy are you with your assessment? Explain. *(Be honest…no one is looking!)*
   a. Energetic and enjoy being around others
   b. Outspoken and often manipulative
   c. Loving, kind and want desperately to be accepted
   d. Intelligent, quiet and prefer to be alone
   e. Other

2. How would others describe you?

3. Do you often feel that you must "wear a mask" when you are around others? If so, explain why? How does it benefit you?

1. **What difference would there be in the way your family/intimates describe you, versus colleagues at your job?**

2. **Which group has the most accurate picture? Explain.**

3. **Unmasked, what are 2-3 of your most important characteristics that you want others to see in you?**

FATT & HAPPY THOUGHT

A grilled cheese sandwich buttered on both sides cooks evenly.
You deserve to be a delicious.
Put down your mask and be AUTHENTICALLY you.

What things will you remember each day this week? What will you see, hear, experience, feel, or do? What will bring warmth, smiles, contentment and joy? Focus Attention and Take Time!

Get FATT & Happy

DAY 64

Feeling highly favored while flawed
Honoring my strengths
Having the fierce conversation
Now It's Your Turn!

1.
2.
3.

DAY 65

All the laundry folded and put away
Patching things up
New affirmations in old books
Now It's Your Turn!

1.
2.
3.

DAY 66

Hand painting book marks
Dancing in between clothes on the line
Watching squirrels darting across the street
Now It's Your Turn!

1.
2.
3.

DAY 67

Good words that become actions
Thankfulness for little things
Wholesome food that tastes good
Now It's Your Turn!

1.
2.
3.

DAY 68

Naming the unborn child
Ice puddles
When someone you love is humble enough to admit they are wrong
Now It's Your Turn!

1.
2.
3.

DAY 69

Old coins with holes
Laying on the beach looking at the sky
Saturday morning blueberry pancakes
Now It's Your Turn!

1.
2.
3.

DAY 70

Fresh fruit in mesh bags
Imagining when Death is no more
Playing flute in public with shaky fingers
Now It's Your Turn!

1.
2.
3.

In the next 3 days, I will ask for help in 1-2 areas where I have needed it the most.

Key 11

GAINING CLARITY:
ARE YOU *REALLY "FINE"*?

Saying "I'm fine", is easier than connecting with how you are really feeling. Have you been dealing with a strange pain, a persistent ache, personal trauma, or other private matters that you won't openly discuss? The tendency to keep them inside makes you feel worse. Without regularly Focusing Attention & Taking Time to assess how you feel, you can miss small emotional and physical ailments that later become serious. Don't do that. You are far too precious. How are you? Get clear.*

**Consider this discovery just a start. If you notice persistent health or emotional concerns, please seek professional medical help. Don't suffer in silence.*

DISCOVERY

1. Sit still for a moment and focus solely on you. Take a few deep breaths and completely relax your body. How do you feel physically? Give yourself an overall rating from 1-5 with 1 being the lowest, and 5 being the highest.

2. If you rated yourself 1-2, is it a physical or emotional pain? Pay attention to your breathing and your heart rate. When you consider how you feel, does your heart rate increase? What area is making you uncomfortable - physical or emotional? Journal about it.

3. Are you taking care of yourself the best* you can? Keeping tabs on your healthcare can reduce stress, especially if you schedule appointments in advance, and then just go! List out the dates of your last regular health visits for the following:
   a. Annual physical _________
   b. Pelvic exam (pap smear, etc) _________
   c. Dental exam _________
   d. Eye exam _________
   e. Full blood panel _________
   f. Mammogram (45+) _________
   g. Colonoscopy (50+) _________
   h. Since you are a *whole* person, why not add the date of the last time you engaged in professional or self-development? It matters!

   ____

If you have other health concerns, don't ignore them. Focus Attention and Take Time. Make appointments as needed.

1. **Having emotional wellness is as important as physical health. What is your emotional state?**
   a. **Unworried and content**
   b. **Optimistic about the future**
   c. **Numb and going through the motions**
   d. **Angry and frustrated**
   e. **Waiting for the worst to happen (fear, worry, anxiety)**
   f. **Other:**

   How long have you been feeling this way?

2. **Is your current/recent emotional status out of the normal for you? If so, who/what contributed to your mindset? If there is a specific event, write about it - positive or negative.**

3. **Physical and emotional health can be present at any weight or age. Make a commitment to be invested in your overall well-being and stay connected to what you *really* feel. To begin, take a few moments to create an intention statement related to your health. Fill in the rest of this statement below:**

   STARTING NOW, I WILL…

FATT & HAPPY THOUGHT

Being just OK isn't enough.
Perfection isn't the goal – Clarity Is.
Seek Clarity.

What things will you remember each day this week? What will you see, hear, experience, feel, or do? What will bring warmth, smiles, contentment and joy? Focus Attention and Take Time!

Get FATT & Happy!

DAY 71

Butterflies before speaking on stage
Bouncing super high balls
Evening ministry
Now It's Your Turn!

1.
2.
3.

DAY 72

Feeling body confident all day
Basketball before breakfast
Dusting the ceiling fan blades
Now It's Your Turn!

1.
2.
3.

DAY 73

Just the right amount of control in your panty hose
Cleansing tea at bedtime
Girls who smile big, proud of their gap
Now It's Your Turn!

1.
2.
3.

DAY 74

Looking through the curtains at the moonlit sky
The first wedding dress
Tarnished sterling silver spoons
Now It's Your Turn!

1.
2.
3.

DAY 75

The sizzle of a warm radiator
A teacup puppy on the end of a long leash
Raking piles of crunchy leaves
Now It's Your Turn!

1.

2.

3.

DAY 76

9 months pregnant and feeling no fear
Strangers with the kind spirit of friends
Cardinals that survive a concussion from flying into the glass door
Now It's Your Turn!

1.

2.

3.

DAY 77

Just one step
Grandmothers crystal goblets
Not having to fold the bedsheets alone
Now It's Your Turn!

1.

2.

3.

This week, I will work hard to substitute negative thoughts with neutral ones.

NOTES

KEY 12

OPEN TO CHANGE

In the simplest terms, change is inevitable. Some changes are good and easy to accept. Others present challenges that throw off your equilibrium. When you have a hard time recalibrating your balance, overwhelm is quick to follow. Being prepared and keeping a positive perspective eases the challenge. Aging is one of the changes that I find hard to accept, both for me and for those I love. It creeps up and you have no choice but to adjust. At first, I was thrown completely off balance by all the little changes. I'm slowly getting used to the new normal. What you face in your life is unique – but change is ever present. The question is: How open are you to change?

1. What is the first thing that comes to your mind when you think about the word "CHANGE"? Do you have a positive or negative first thought? Explain.

2. Regardless of your present age, as a woman, you are in the process of change. Think puberty, pregnancy, etc. What physical changes are you currently experiencing? How are you coping with these changes?

3. Journal about one AMAZING change that you experienced in the past 12 months. If there was a transition in how you felt initially, be sure to include that detail. How did your perspective help? What were the benefits of accepting this change?

1. Being open to change is not the same thing as going from one thing to another to avoid making a decision work. When have you made a quick decision to change, just so that you could avoid a painful (growth) opportunity?

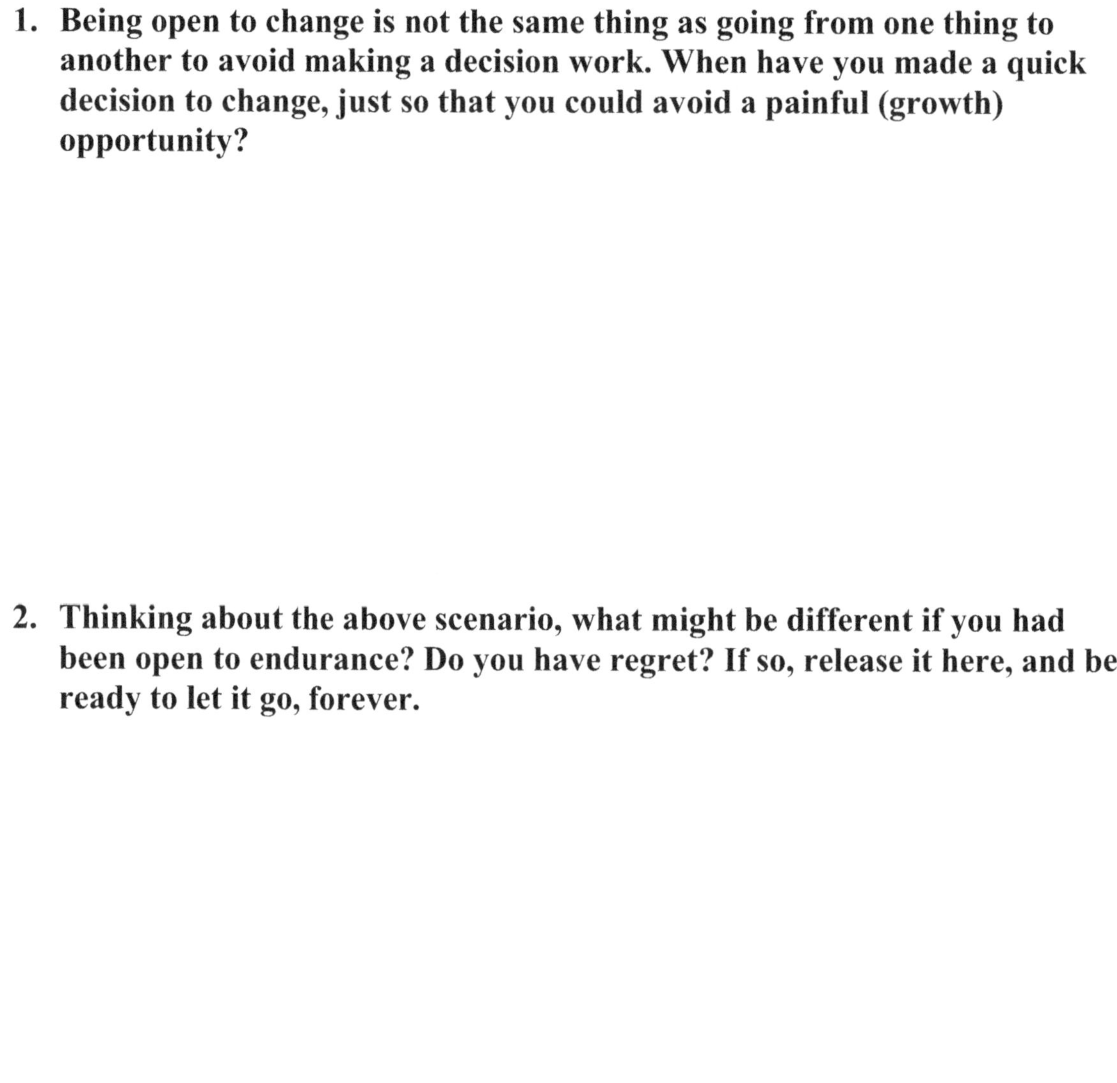

2. Thinking about the above scenario, what might be different if you had been open to endurance? Do you have regret? If so, release it here, and be ready to let it go, forever.

Being open to sensitive and personal changes takes commitment. A relative gets sick and you become the caretaker. Your parents are aging and need your help financially. You love your husband, but the relationship is rocky. You take on a new team at work; they don't like you and you are pretty sure the feeling is mutual. You need to lose over 100 pounds because you have developed a health condition, but you don't want to let go of the foods and lifestyle routines that are no longer serving you. Your list will be different. Be honest with yourself and keep your perspective as positive as possible. Change is completely unavoidable and often unannounced. Feeling bad about it is a choice.

FATT & HAPPY THOUGHT

**Every change you have endured has made you a much stronger woman. Don't forget:
Strength is Beautiful!**

What things will you remember each day this week? What will you see, hear, experience, feel, or do? What will bring warmth, smiles, contentment and joy? Focus Attention and Take Time!

Get FATT & Happy!

DAY 78

Bags of crabapples from LaGrange, GA
Having no need to prove anything
Pomegranate and beet juice residue on my lips
Now It's Your Turn!

1.
2.
3.

DAY 79

Being inspired by a workshop
Making eye contact with a horse
Drinking ginger peach tea
Now It's Your Turn!

1.
2.
3.

DAY 80

An easy-open box of spring mix salad
Running my feet against the carpet grain
Picking out clothes for picture day
Now It's Your Turn!

1.
2.
3.

DAY 81

A warm welcome someplace new
Perfect lift from a perfect bra
Being chased by a dog and happy about it
Now It's Your Turn!

1.
2.
3.

DAY 82

Making sure they pronounce my name
Getting the first gas pump at Costco
Extra virgin olive oil, garlic, lemon, and fresh thyme
Now It's Your Turn!

1.

2.

3.

DAY 83

Saturday morning 'Soul Train' memories
Old friends who know me well
Finding peace while waiting in line
Now It's Your Turn!

1.

2.

3.

DAY 84

Baristas that call you by name
Finding your lost sunglasses your head
Polo shirts with firm collars after 100 washes
Now It's Your Turn!

1.

2.

3.

This week, I will purge 3 items from my closet that no longer fit, I no longer wear, or that bring unwelcome thoughts to my mind.

NOTES

KEY 13

GAINING CLARITY:
ARE YOU EASILY INTIMIDATED?

In the simplest terms, to be intimidated means to feel timid, or to feel fear. You may feel intimated by a person, by a situation or even by a set of circumstances. Although anyone can feel this at any time, women are the most likely victims. Over time, fearfulness can result in a feeling of powerlessness subtly influencing every part of life. There is no clarity or peace in powerlessness.

**Intimidation as discussed here does not refer to physical, mental or sexual abuse. However, do use Key 13 to identify this kind of intimidation as well, and then please seek the support of a professional.*

1. In your life, when do you feel the most intimidated? Who are you afraid to upset? What situations make you feel nervous? (Go ahead, It's OK to name them.)
   a. At work
   b. At home
   c. In everyday dealings
   d. Extended family home life

2. If you are intimidated by a person that you know well, do you think this person knows what they are doing? Do *you* believe that it is deliberate? (Please explain.)

3. Think about it. Is this person someone that other people also fear, or is your intimidation due to habit? Explain.

1. **Think about a time when you were intimidated, but instead of cowering back in fear, you spoke up for yourself and showed courage. How did it feel and how did others respond?**

2. **If you are in the midst of an intimidating situation, what is the most uncomfortable thing about it? If you confronted this head-on, write out the best scenario. Conversely, what do you think is the worst that could happen?**

3. **In the next 7-10 days, what is one thing you can do to release the hold this person or situation has on you? How will that win feel?**

FATT & HAPPY THOUGHT

Often times people who knowingly intimidate have a strong desire to feel important and a basic need to control others.
Does that sound happy to you?
Be Authentic. Be Yourself. Be Happy.

What things will you remember each day this week? What will you see, hear, experience, feel, or do? What will bring warmth, smiles, contentment and joy? Focus Attention and Take Time!

Get FATT & Happy!

DAY 85

Finding a good dollar store novel
Pitching the first spring tent
Cartoon band-aids
Now It's Your Turn!

1.

2.

3.

DAY 86

Looking at photos of a newly blind photographer
Zucchini grilled on skewers, sprinkled with sea salt
Watching toads catch their evening buffet
Now It's Your Turn!

1.

2.

3.

DAY 87

Shaking pompoms for the winning team
Welcome home banners at the airport
Walking silently on a hiking trail
Now It's Your Turn!

1.

2.

3.

DAY 88

Licking the drop of syrup from my pinky
Watching my son put rosin on his cello bow
Ordering in gluten-free pizza
Now It's Your Turn!

1.

2.

3.

DAY 89

Napping in the parking lot
Tidying up the linen closet
Fresh baked dinosaur kale
Now It's Your Turn!

1.
2.
3.

DAY 90

Well-worn tennis shoes
12 step coins
When someone comes back for you
Now It's Your Turn!

1.
2.
3.

DAY 91

Engagement parties
Being invested in being confident
The sound of my flip-flops on the boardwalk
Now It's Your Turn!

1.
2.
3.

Discovery: This week, I will make a list of my growth and accomplishments from the last 30 day

Key 14

You Deserve to Take Up Space

This conversation starts with weight and body size, but that only scratches the surface. Only recently has it become acceptable for a woman to be "weighty" in body and mind. The disconnect in deserve level lingers. It does not have to linger in you.

In this exact moment, would you say that you approve of the amount of space that your body is using? I'm not saying that you love being petite and small, or that you adore your round belly and hips. But right here in this moment, can you nod your head and agree that you deserve to take up space without needing to apologize for it?

Taking up space involves the depth of your voice, your ideas, your dreams, your intentions, and yes – your body. You deserve respect no matter what your size or shape. And if you want that respect from others, it must start with you. Give yourself permission to take up space. Start Here.

1. **Regardless of how you feel about your body size, do you agree that your talents, ideas, qualities are the most important parts of you? If you don't agree, why not?**

2. **Finish this sentence, and then journal.** *When I enter a room, people . . .*
   a. **Enjoy my company and want to be with me**
   b. **Think my personality is "too much" for them**
   c. **Tolerate me due to obligation**
   d. **Are embarrassed by me**

3. **Write your affirmational "Deserve Level" statement below.**

   Regardless of my many imperfections both physically and emotionally, I deserve to take up space because...

CONSIDER

1. **With whom in your life do you feel 100% comfortable? For example, regardless of the circumstance, they will respect who you are, what you believe in, how you think, and do not care how you look?**

2. **How do you feel about the size of your body? Do you think it gives or takes away your personal power? (Choose one and review the tips below.)**
   a. **My body size makes me feel authoritative and powerful because I am tall. Most times I like it.**
   b. **Sometimes my larger size makes me feel awkward.**
   c. **I am small and sometimes I feel ignored or treated like a child.**
   d. **I accept myself and my body. I don't think it influences my credibility or the respect I receive from others.**

TIPS ON MANAGING FEELINGS ABOUT YOUR SIZE

A. If you feel that your size is towering and adds to your power in a negative way, be sure your communication style is kind and accepting. This will ensure that others see you as approachable.

B. If you feel awkward due to being a larger size, be sure your posture is erect or you will look insecure. Your unique interest, non-biased judgment & knowledge can easily give you personal power.

C. If you have the tendency to feel overlooked due to your small size, be sure that you ask directly for what you want, don't whine when you talk, and don't over-explain your answers. Your communication style can make your smallness BIG.

D. Your size doesn't add or take away your power. What you say and how you say it, is what others will notice most about you. As mentioned in Key 5, also allow your style of dress to increase your personal power.

See Additional Resources to learn more strategies.

FATT & HAPPY THOUGHT

The typical size of most people is getter larger, not smaller. And yet the conversation is far deeper than size. Regardless of the weight and stature of your body, it's the weight and stature of your inner person that makes the biggest impact.

What things will you remember each day this week? What will you see, hear, experience, feel, or do? What will bring warmth, smiles, contentment and joy? Focus Attention and Take Time!

Get FATT & Happy!

DAY 92

Single lane bridges
One plain donut dunked in hot coffee
The narrow streets of historic Ellicott City, Maryland
Now It's Your Turn!

1.

2.

3.

DAY 93

Watching TV until midnight
Dark green grass peeking through the snow
Eating out in the open
Now It's Your Turn!

1.

2.

3.

DAY 94

Red barn doors
Rocking chairs outside of Cracker Barrel™
Surgeons playing Vivaldi while they work
Now It's Your Turn!

1.

2.

3.

DAY 95

Checking on the kids one last time
The rise and fall of a fur-baby's belly
Dusting the mini blinds
Now It's Your Turn!

1.

2.

3.

DAY 96
Natural hair wrapped tall in Kente cloth
Two extra hours of sleep
Floor-length curtains in pastel prints
Now It's Your Turn!

1.

2.

3.

DAY 97
Napping before dinner with your baby
Taking your great-grandmother to breakfast
Gently rubbing the bruise until you don't feel it anymore
Now It's Your Turn!

1.

2.

3.

DAY 98
Packing for a long-awaited trip
First spring flowers
Loving the girl that stares back at you
Now It's Your Turn!

1.

2.

3.

Starting this week, I will let go of comparing myself to others.

NOTES

Key 15

Over Apologizing

Over apologizing is a mode of communication based on an underlying sense of wanting to please. It's often used by women who struggle to maintain boundaries or have an over-active sense of kindness and compassion. It can become a reflexive way to express oneself that adds little to the conversation and can eventually cheapen a relationship. Unintentionally, this is a quick way for a woman to lose power and respect, especially in business. Instead of 'sounding nicer' it suggests a lack of confidence and worthiness to openly share ideas. Do you over apologize? If so, feel free to stop now.

1. In what circumstances do you over apologize? Explain.
    a. When I'm nervous
    b. When I'm around strangers
    c. Only on a rare occasion, for example, if I try to comfort someone who is sick, or grieving
    d. I don't struggle with this

2. If you answered "c" or "d", what qualities do you have that prevent you from over apologizing? If you answered "a" or "b", what qualities do you have that cause your tendency to over apologize?

3. How do you feel when someone repeatedly says, 'I'm sorry', even when you both know there is no basis for the apology? How does it make you feel?

1. When others have over apologized to you, has this helped or hurt the communication in the relationship? Explain.

2. If you recognize that you have a habit of over apologizing, how ready are you to move toward a more meaningful, productive, and impactful way of communicating your thoughts and feelings? Rate your readiness to change with 1 being the lowest and 5 being the highest. Explain your rating.

3. Pause. Think of your relationships, both intimates and acquaintances. Does anyone owe you an apology, but has withheld it? How do you feel about it? And what about you? Instead of excusing yourself, who deserves your apology? This week, can you take care of this? Journal and Get Ready.

FATT & HAPPY THOUGHT

If you feel the need to apologize or say, 'I'm sorry', pause and think about what you really mean. Say that instead. Watch change happen.

What things will you remember each day this week? What will you see, hear, experience, feel, or do? What will bring warmth, smiles, contentment and joy? Focus Attention and Take Time!

Get FATT & Happy!

DAY 99

Acoustic guitar strumming in the background
Mailing a condolence card
Quiet moments just before the kids wake
Now It's Your Turn!

1.
2.
3.

DAY 100

Checking in
A blank canvas and clean brushes
Red throated woodpeckers in the front yard
Now It's Your Turn!

1.
2.
3.

DAY 101

Getting a splinter with a needle just like mom
Flexible bosses
When strangers smile with their eyes
Now It's Your Turn!

1.
2.
3.

DAY 102

Brave tweens who put themselves "out there"
The 10th of June
Music booster parents
Now It's Your Turn!

1.
2.
3.

DAY 103

The last box unpacked
Motivation from within to get the work out
1-3 inches instead of 6-8
Now It's Your Turn!

1.

2.

3.

DAY 104

Finding a safety pin at the bottom of your purse
Cookies for breakfast
Three bright red birds on one skinny branch
Now It's Your Turn!

1.

2.

3.

DAY 105

Black and white striped maxi dresses
The first pink moon of spring
Fuchsia pedicure
Now It's Your Turn!

1.

2.

3.

I will eat only when I am hungry for at least 2 days this week. I will feed my mind every day.

Key 16

Guarding Personal Boundaries

Personal boundaries are the limits you create to be safe. As women, our vulnerability can be a major asset. It can also turn quickly into a liability if we don't set rules for what we will accept from other people. As a recovering people pleaser, I have experienced how it feels to let folks stomp all over my boundaries with total disregard. It feels terrible. How people talk to you, touch you, treat you, even what they call you, is wrapped in the boundaries you set and keep for yourself.*
Are you guarding your boundaries?

When it comes to personal boundaries, there are 2 types of challenging groups of people:
1. *Those you chose to be around*
2. *Those who have to be in your life due to work, family dynamics or day-to-day obligations*

Set your boundaries accordingly!

1. In what relationship or situation do you need to set better boundaries? Is there anyone in your life (by choice) from whom you need to distance yourself? Who is it, and why?

2. What are you doing that activates and feeds into this relationship? (Example: initiating phone calls, acting like you feel a strong connection when you really do not, etc.)

3. In Key 13 you identified intimidating people in your life. Is this the same person? If so, what's holding you back from creating safer boundaries?

CONSIDER

1. **Create a list. What situations/relationships are you maintaining where you need to establish better personal boundaries?**

   a.

   b.

   c.

   d.

   e.

2. **Examine the above list. Is there a close family member or friend listed? What are 3 things you can do to foster a balanced relationship, and still maintain your personal boundaries? How willing are you implement at least 3 things?**

   a.

   b.

   c.

   How willing are you implement at least 3 things?

3. **Although you cannot eliminate every challenging relationship, if you know in your gut that your boundaries are time and again being violated, it's time to take action. Focus Attention. Take Time. Do the work. How would it feel if you gave yourself permission to create wholesome and healthy personal boundaries, and then stick to them? What are 2 things you can gently start doing in the next 7-10 days to establish distance without animosity?**

   a.

   b.

142

FATT & HAPPY THOUGHT

You are more worthy of honor than you imagine.

What things will you remember each day this week? What will you see, hear, experience, feel, or do? What will bring warmth, smiles, contentment and joy? Focus Attention and Take Time!

Get FATT & Happy!

DAY 106

Fried cauliflower rice
Young boys on strings
Talking in a British accent all day
Now It's Your Turn!

1.

2.

3.

DAY 107

Building with Legos ™
The 8+ year light bulb in the closet
Waking before the alarm and feeling rested
Now It's Your Turn!

1.

2.

3.

DAY 108

Kind radiology technicians
Apples with a leaf stem
Addressing envelopes in line at the post office
Now It's Your Turn!

1.

2.

3.

DAY 109

City pigeons visiting the rooftop during dinner
Throwing my toys out of the pram
Praying on behalf of someone who asks for it
Now It's Your Turn!

1.

2.

3.

DAY 110

Warm cornbread
Lemongrass oil
Baby lambs following their momma
Now It's Your Turn!

1.

2.

3.

DAY 111

Puddles beneath my feet
One B amid straight A's
Running through a warm rain
Now It's Your Turn!

1.

2.

3.

DAY 112

Reading by an open window
Writing signature poems for strangers
Public displays of affection
Now It's Your Turn!

1.

2.

3.

This week I will stare into the mirror and repeat:
"I Am Beautiful"

NOTES

Key 17

Say What Needs to Be Said

When I was working in the corporate space, there was one time in particular that I felt completely dejected because of receiving a demotion I did not deserve. There was no heads-up or warning. I found out in a public meeting, at the same time as my team, when the presentation slide came across the screen. My entire team had been assigned to someone yet to be hired. When I spoke up later that day, I embarrassed myself. I blubbered a bit, and it was hard to get through – but I said what I needed to say. Eleven months later, there was a request to restore my former position at the same salary. There was yet another conversation, where I had to say exactly what was on my mind, despite being afraid. That time it worked in my favor.

Intimidation. Lost personal boundaries. Energy draining relationships. Overwork. Feeling disrespected. Not liking yourself enough. All of these cause silence.

One of the biggest stressors you will ever encounter is a silent, self-inflicted one. When you hold back from telling the truth, you lose your peace. Eventually among those who matter most, you may even lose your 'right' to voice your thoughts. No amount of FATT & Happy can change that. Conflict continues with closed mouths. Resolution begins with the truth. What do you need to say?

1. Think about your spouse, children and other intimate relationships. Is there an elephant in the room? What do you need to clarify so you can live in authenticity?

2. Think about your workplace. What do you need to address to clear up misunderstandings with your team, colleagues, department heads, and yes, even your boss? Make a list of the top 2-3 things you need to discuss and set a specific date to have the conversations.

3. When you think about your overall communication, how open and honest are you? How often does fear of conflict or hurting someone's feelings cause you to "coat" the truth?

1. Who do you know that is a strong communicator and makes an effort to be honest and authentic when dealing with others, even when it's not easy?

2. If any of the issues you need to address stem from a misunderstanding that you created, what has held you back from addressing it? And on a scale of 1-5, with 5 being the most, how ready are you to seek resolution?

3. Above all else, what unresolved issue is causing you the most stress and frustration? *Address this with urgency.*

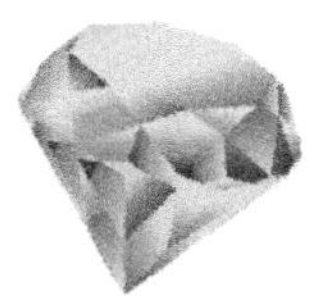

FATT & HAPPY THOUGHT

Being authentic and honest can often be challenging. It has nothing to do with being the oldest or having the most prominent role. It takes courage. Remember: You Are Brave!

What things will you remember each day this week? What will you see, hear, experience, feel, or do? What will bring warmth, smiles, contentment and joy? Focus Attention and Take Time!

Get FATT & Happy!

DAY 113

House music and dancing on Saturday night
Balsamic rice vinegar on spring mix
Old stone archways
Now It's Your Turn!

1.
2.
3.

DAY 114

8 hours of uninterrupted sleep
A1C on the decline
Getting invited
Now It's Your Turn!

1.
2.
3.

DAY 115

Sparrows collecting twigs
A flock of geese in formation
Hot pink Converse high tops with yellow laces
Now It's Your Turn!

1.
2.
3.

DAY 116

When mommies come back home
When the long-awaited cycle comes
Releasing the traumatic event
Now It's Your Turn!

1.
2.
3.

DAY 117

Sneaking a little cake batter from a wooden spoon
Staying inside on a rainy day
A bright idea that works
Now It's Your Turn!

1.

2.

3.

DAY 118

Getting the first AM appointment
Making snow angels in the middle of the street
Pumice stones on my feet
Now It's Your Turn!

1.

2.

3.

DAY 119

Super fine tip roller ball pens
Playing catch with my son
Greek yogurt topped with granola in a blue bowl
Now It's Your Turn!

1.

2.

3.

This week, I will speak up respectfully at work.
I will use my voice. I will share my ideas.

NOTES

Key 18

The Art of Saying "No"

When you say 'yes' to one thing, you automatically say 'no' to something else. Saying yes to the wrong things can rain down havoc on your personal boundaries, your relationships, your job and sometimes your entire life. No, is a complete sentence. Learning to say it with grace is an art worth developing. When you Focus Attention & Take Time this week, spend a few moments thinking about if you need to use this full sentence more often.

1. Do you find that you have a pattern saying of "yes", when you are fully aware that you should say "no"? When and why have you allowed this pattern to develop?

2. Are more likely to agree to things at work, or at home? Which place do you feel the strongest need to please?

3. If your friends or colleagues ask more of you than they do of others, do you feel it's because they know you will say "yes"? Explain.

1. **Think back to the last time you inappropriately agreed to something. What would have happened if you had declined?**

2. **Make a list of things are you currently agreeing to that you need to start declining? How do you feel about letting go?**

3. **Growing your self-worth and knowing that your time and priorities matter will help you practice self-care in the area of saying "no". One effective strategy is to pause when answering. *Mine the gap* and genuinely think how you can respect your time, energy and limitations. *Then* answer. How would it feel to do this?   Brainstorm a few strategies and write them below. *Write down only what you think you can actually implement within the next 2 weeks.***

FATT & HAPPY THOUGHT

**Value your time. Know your priorities.
Owning your "No" is an act of self-care.**

What things will you remember each day this week? What will you see, hear, experience, feel, or do? What will bring warmth, smiles, contentment and joy? Focus Attention and Take Time!

Get FATT & Happy!

DAY 120

Crossed legs and high heel pumps
Dark chocolate power berries
Cooling the apple juice outside on the deck
Now It's Your Turn!

1.

2.

3.

DAY 121

Sharing earphones
Sun breaking through a cloudy sky
A perfect cabernet in a short fat glass
Now It's Your Turn!

1.

2.

3.

DAY 122

Watching steam rise from the soup pot
Companionable silence
The 2nd of June
Now It's Your Turn!

1.

2.

3.

DAY 123

Smoothies in the afternoon
Nurses that check after minor procedures
The whole family watching The Ravens
Now It's Your Turn!

1.

2.

3.

DAY 124

Planning a surprise for someone you love
Friendly haggling
Monday night half-price spaghetti
Now It's Your Turn!

1.

2.

3.

DAY 125

Extra long spoons
Paint by numbers
Finding the last puzzle piece
Now It's Your Turn!

1.

2.

3.

DAY 126

Paint swatches
Climbing up to the backyard treehouse
Genuine childhood innocence
Now It's Your Turn!

1.

2.

3.

This week, I will practice self-care by declining what I know will stretch me beyond what I can healthily do.

Key 19

Sweet Talk Your Self Talk

Each of us is like a beautiful silk gown. How we talk to ourselves is the difference between placing that gown on a velvet hanger in a moth-free dress bag or throwing it on the floor and walking on it with dirty boots. Self-talk is the internal dialogue that is positive and supportive, or negative and self-defeating. It underscores whether you see yourself as good, worthy and capable, or undeserving, incompetent and not good enough. Are you sweet talking your self-talk?

1. **The Tone of Your Self-Talk. What kinds of things do you say to yourself? Is your self-talk primarily positive or negative? Write down a few examples of what you say to yourself. If you aren't sure, pay attention over the next few days, then revisit and journal.**

2. **Whether positive or negative, do you remember any specific circumstances related to "early" self-talk in your life? If negative, was it related to a member of your family? Be specific.**

3. **Journal for a few moments. When do you tend to self-criticize? Is the reason externally or internally triggered? Now, what about self-congratulation? When and why are you motivated to give yourself a pat on the back?**

1. If you struggle with negative self-talk, perhaps putting yourself down about your weight, appearance, relationship or career, how open are you to changing this habit?

2. The next time you find yourself engaging in negative self-talk or self-defeating thoughts, how could you reframe the conversation? For example: "Things never work out for me! I should just give up!" Practice creating a *realistic* reframe below.

3. Imagine if you were to conquer negative self-talk. How would you feel? What would be different in your everyday life?

FATT & HAPPY THOUGHT

You are blessed with 60,000+ thoughts every day. Be the exception and let yours reign with positivity!

What things will you remember each day this week? What will you see, hear, experience, feel, or do? What will bring warmth, smiles, contentment and joy? Focus Attention and Take Time!

Get FATT & Happy!

DAY 127
Being less afraid to do new things
Using my imagination
Humming along to Bollywood songs
Now It's Your Turn!

1.

2.

3.

DAY 128
Jazzercise™ class
Breathlessness while working out
Letting someone worthy in
Now It's Your Turn!

1.

2.

3.

DAY 129
American Sign Language poetry
Significant bible collections
Finding the favorite book, I thought was lost
Now It's Your Turn!

1.

2.

3.

DAY 130
Collard greens softly cooked
The fading scent of cedar
Elaborate multi-colored Victorian homes
Now It's Your Turn!

1.

2.

3.

DAY 131

Wayne & Mary Ellen's twin girls, Samantha & Sophia
Creating dinner from next to nothing
Eggs any and every time of day
Now It's Your Turn!

1.

2.

3.

DAY 132

Blogs that celebrate family life
Previous century family photographs
Frosting cupcakes
Now It's Your Turn!

1.

2.

3.

DAY 133

A woman's jiggle in high-heeled boots
Speaking up for what I believe
Supporting your spouse
Now It's Your Turn!

1.

2.

3.

Discovery: This week, I will make a list of my growth and accomplishments from the last 30 days.

NOTES

Key 20

Forgive & Move On

Forgiving is better for you than for the other person. No one doubts the validity of moving on, and no one wants to be stuck in negative energy that has no end. Does this include you? Absolutely! Forgiveness delivers more dividends and opens far more doors when it's related to your own mistakes and misgivings. It's hard to witness even the simplest happiness when you refuse to see past what you've done wrong. But that's what this journey is about. Girl, you can do hard things! Do you need to forgive yourself for something and finally move on?

1. **What does forgiveness mean to you? Do you view it as a sign of strength or weakness? Explain.**

2. **How well do you forgive others? Rate yourself on a scale of 1-5 with 5 being the best. Why do you answer that way? If there is someone you need to forgive right now – write their name below. *(Real forgiveness means that you don't continue to think about it or repeatedly reflect on it.)***

3. **How well do you forgive yourself? What are you holding onto right now that you need to release and forgive yourself for doing, saying, or being?**

1. Do you have a tendency to hold onto your mistakes well past when you should release them? How might your life be different if you started forgiving yourself for minor things and then working to deal with the major things?

2. It's often hard to let go of past occurrences that were out of your control – like having been violated in some way. Guilt and shame are the result. This can leave a stain that remains and is very challenging to remove without help. If you have been violated in some way *and feel ready* to move on, what steps* can you take in the next 7-10 days?

If negative feelings persist, please consider seeking professional assistance.

FATT & HAPPY THOUGHT

Forgiving someone does not mean you have to invite them fully back into your life. That's a choice you get to make. But when you forgive YOURSELF, you get to finally accept the lesson and release the negativity so your positivity can reign again.

What things will you remember each day this week? What will you see, hear, experience, feel, or do? What will bring warmth, smiles, contentment and joy? Focus Attention and Take Time!

Get FATT & Happy

DAY 134
Drying our own garlic
Finally letting it go
Cinnamon sticks boiling on the stove
Now It's Your Turn!

1.

2.

3.

DAY 135
My boys beatboxing in the dark
Listening to my parents' love story
Napping in a hammock
Now It's Your Turn!

1.

2.

3.

DAY 136
Being the incentive
Receiving the incentive
Lipstick affirmations on bathroom mirrors
Now It's Your Turn!

1.

2.

3.

DAY 137
Natural hair in joyful transition
Admiring your thighs in plus sized jeans
Teaching kids my favorite old songs
Now It's Your Turn!

1.

2.

3.

DAY 138

Being the mom who picks up after school
Bedtime (enough said)
Second grade spelling bees
Now It's Your Turn!

1.

2.

3.

DAY 139

Downton Abbey's, Lady Mary
Not blending in
Hula-hooping for 10 minutes straight
Now It's Your Turn!

1.

2.

3.

DAY 140

Grilled salmon over an open fire
Nude matte lipstick
Al denté pasta
Now It's Your Turn!

1.

2.

3.

This week, I will forgive myself for not moving on sooner.

Key 21

Food, Eating & Shame

Shame is an intense pain associated with feeling flawed. It can stem from an experience or imagined experience where one feels unworthy of love, unworthy of belonging or even of existing. If the relationship with your weight or body image has been a turbulent one, eating may become a shameful act. In general, women tend to hide what they eat far more often than men. Hiding an action, as necessary as eating, causes an ongoing cycle of shame. All the while, eating can be one of many simple pleasures that we can enjoy - No Shame Required.
*What is **your** relationship with eating and food?*

**If you feel that you have a serious issue with disordered eating, please consider professional help. You deserve to be happy. If you have another secret shame or hidden activity, substitute your answers on the following pages.*

1. Do you hide or conceal what or how much or little you eat? If yes, where do you feel most comfortable eating?
   a. Yes, constantly (several times a week)
   b. Often (a few times a month)
   c. Occasionally (only when I'm with people I don't know well)
   d. Never, I eat what I want, whenever I want

2. If you feel the need to hide, what is the reason? For example, do you feel silently judged or have a fear of verbal attack? Explain.

3. What foods do you feel uncomfortable eating in front of other people? Journal on any experience (past or recent) that triggers this feeling.

1. What is the worst part of eating alone and out of sight of others? What is your favorite part?

2. If you feel that someone is quietly judging you, are they generally judgmental? If so, how can you use this knowledge in your own personal defense?

3. Create a scenario where you are eating exactly what you want with friends, family, strangers, or anyone else where you might have previously felt shame. In this scenario no one notices you, your body, your plate, and in the case of friends, just the conversation and the meal itself is important. Write about how this experience feels.

FATT & HAPPY THOUGHT

The shame is not in eating, but in silence.
Hunger in the heart leads to growling in the soul.
It's OK to let it go.

What things will you remember each day this week? What will you see, hear, experience, feel, or do? What will bring warmth, smiles, contentment and joy? Focus Attention and Take Time!

Get FATT & Happy

DAY 141

Pointy black cowboy boots accented in teal blue
Fat and fragrant lemons
Hot water from a frozen tap
Now It's Your Turn!

1.

2.

3.

DAY 142

Cooking bacon just outside a tent
Cars that start when it's 2 degrees
Smiling kids getting off a yellow school bus
Now It's Your Turn!

1.

2.

3.

DAY 143

Movie popcorn
Dads writing school notes
Working out at every size
Now It's Your Turn!

1.

2.

3.

DAY 144

Letting go of the past
5-year-old yoga pants
Successful and short business meetings
Now It's Your Turn!

1.

2.

3.

DAY 145
Watching America's Funniest Videos
Knowing before you "know"
Being surprised when the unexpected shows up
Now It's Your Turn!

1.

2.

3.

DAY 146
Collaboration
Peets Cafe Domingo
Conversation and a bottomless pot of diner coffee
Now It's Your Turn!

1.

2.

3.

DAY 147
Tires rolling along gravelly roads
Fuzzy caterpillars running in the grass
The 14th of April
Now It's Your Turn!

1.

2.

3.

This week, I will take a stand against body, weight and food shaming – starting with me.

NOTES

Key 22

It's Not as Personal as You Think

My mom used to say: "Girl, stop taking it all so personally!" It took me until well into my 30s to understand what she meant. But she knew what she was talking about. Momma was right!

Sensitivity is one a woman's gifts. It helps us to be tender mothers and caring wives. It enables us to see hidden aspects of risky business deals. In proper measure, it allows us to go deeper on issues that matter. However, taking things too personally, clouds thinking, drains energy, and causes us to be over-critical of ourselves and suspicious of others. Have you been accused of taking things too personally?
If so, let's see how to adjust that right now.

1. On average, how would you rate your level of sensitivity? Do you notice minor mistakes in others at home or at work? Do seemingly small things rob your peace of mind? If yes, why?

2. Under what circumstances are you the most sensitive? Note a recent example when someone told you that you were being too sensitive. Explore.
   a. Work with colleagues
   b. Home with kids, extended family
   c. Intimate relationships

3. In what way has your sensitivity helped your relationships? In what way has it damaged your relationships? (Think about all of the relationships mentioned above.)

1. When you are hyper-sensitive and take everything personally, you rob yourself of inner peace and create tense relationships. How important is your peace of mind?

2. Instead of questioning or guessing the motives and intentions of others when certain situations come up, what strategies can you use to neutralize your feelings?

3. If you have a tendency to be overly critical with yourself, how can you employ the same strategies you would with others, to enhance the relationship you have with yourself?

FATT & HAPPY THOUGHT

When you are ready to change your life bad enough, you can break through any cycle of disempowerment. Believe it.

What things will you remember each day this week? What will you see, hear, experience, feel, or do? What will bring warmth, smiles, contentment and joy? Focus Attention and Take Time!

Get FATT & Happy!

DAY 148

Cold feet on ceramic tile by a winter window
Powerful anonymous quotes
Honey Dijon mustard dip
Now It's Your Turn!

1.

2.

3.

DAY 149

Sleeping late
71-degree February days
Allowing yourself to drive and get lost
Now It's Your Turn!

1.

2.

3.

DAY 150

Taking a long bubble bath with candles
Walking in the park listening to your favorite song
Joyously satisfying a big appetite
Now It's Your Turn!

1.

2.

3.

DAY 151

Your favorite team winning the Super Bowl
Getting an unexpected dinner out
Putting gold stars on the calendar
Now It's Your Turn!

1.

2.

3.

DAY 152
Completely free Saturday afternoons
Using your eyelashes to put the baby to sleep
Cleaning fish on the back deck
Now It's Your Turn!

1.

2.

3.

DAY 153
Going up a dress size and still feeling gorgeous
Perusing library bookshelves
Kids that use"eeny meeny, miney, mo" to choose teams
Now It's Your Turn!

1.

2.

3.

DAY 154
Crossed arm confidence, with outstretched arms
Comfortable heels
5000-piece puzzles ten minutes at a time
Now It's Your Turn!

1.

2.

3.

This week, I will encourage someone who needs it by calling, sending a text, writing a card, or stopping by their home.

Key 23

Discover Your Gifts

Gifts are the natural talents that you do without thinking. They are clearly found in childhood, and often overlooked in adulthood. Women easily identify them in other people, but not as often in themselves. Finding them, enhancing them and using them can ease your life both at work and at home. Go discover your gifts!

1. What is one thing you have always done naturally well? Although this is a natural ability, is it something you enjoy? (For example; You are a good leader, but don't like to be in charge.)

2. What ability have others recognized in you? Is it the same or different?

3. Make a list of 5-10 of your personal gifts/natural abilities. Include hard and soft skills.
   a.
   b.
   c.
   d.
   e.
   f.
   g.
   h.
   i.
   j.

1. Pick one of the gifts you listed that you are not currently using on a regular basis. How can you incorporate it into your daily routine in the next 7-10 days?

2. How confident are you with speaking up about your natural abilities at work in meetings, on interviews or in seeking out new opportunities as an entrepreneur? Even if you have avoided it in the past, how might being assertive in this way help you?

3. How can you specifically use your emotional gifts to strengthen your relationships both at home and in your work?

FATT & HAPPY THOUGHT

You are not too old, and it is not too late. You have many gifts.
Now is the time. Find them. Share them.
So many people are waiting.

What things will you remember each day this week? What will you see, hear, experience, feel, or do? What will bring warmth, smiles, contentment and joy? Focus Attention and Take Time!

Get FATT & Happy!

DAY 155

Being forgiven
A kitten chasing a bright ball of yarn
The smell of chocolate chip cookies baking
Now It's Your Turn!

1.

2.

3.

DAY 156

The perfect gym shoes
A traffic-free commute to work
Your son texting that he loves you
Now It's Your Turn!

1.

2.

3.

DAY 157

Loving your favorite person
Losing 10 pounds without noticing
When your adult daughter crawls into bed with you
Now It's Your Turn!

1.

2.

3.

DAY 158

Watching a wedding photo shoot
Making a new friend
Blessing someone just by smiling
Now It's Your Turn!

1.

2.

3.

DAY 159

Being told I am special
Groceries being half the price you expected
Blowing bubbles in the front yard
Now It's Your Turn!

1.

2.

3.

DAY 160

Giggling in public
Grandmother's pear pie
Running into your 7th grade English teacher
Now It's Your Turn!

1.

2.

3.

DAY 161

Accepting an apology
The perfect puppy
Feeling especially beautiful
Now It's Your Turn!

1.

2.

3.

**This week, I will give my most important relationship
more of the real me.**

Key 24

Make Time for Self-Care

Self-care is no longer a luxury. It's not just long days at a spa or expensive vacations with girlfriends. It's a necessity for busy women so they can keep going strong. This is one of the keys to avoiding burnout. You can't wait for just a few times a year. You have to make time.

24. 7. 365. We all get the same amount of time. It's not about how much you have. It's about how much you spend, how much you lose, how much you balance, how much you save.

To create room for self-care, you have to be in choice about your schedule, your commitments and if you will give yourself permission to put yourself back on the list and take care of YOU!*

**See the additional resources section of this book for a list of self-care ideas*

DISCOVERY

1. List the first 5 things that come to mind when you hear "self-care"?
    a.
    b.
    c.
    d.
    e.

    When is the last time you engaged in one of these activities?

2. What stands in the way when it comes to your confident self-care? And how likely would you be to practice regular self-care if those obstacles were out of the way. (Be honest.)

3. Down deep, do you feel that self-care is selfish or unimportant? Why or why not?

1. What are 5 things* you could do in 10 minutes or less each day to enhance your self-care regime?
   a.
   b.
   c.
   d.
   e.

2. Women who regularly practice self-care have less stress, look younger, sleep better, live longer, and generally have better work-life balance. Which of these would you like increase in your life? How willing are you to refresh your commitment to taking better care of yourself?

3. Commitment Time! Pick a day/date and put it on your calendar. Use a gold star, a special ink marker or setup a fun alarm on your smart device. Tell someone who will hold you accountable to your actions. Outline what you will do, how you will prepare, and then write about how good you will feel, as if you have already done it. Go!

FATT & HAPPY THOUGHT

Giving yourself permission to pause is so much better than expecting yourself to keep going no matter what.
Take time to rejuvenate and refresh!

What things will you remember each day this week? What will you see, hear, experience, feel, or do? What will bring warmth, smiles, contentment and joy? Focus Attention and Take Time!

Get FATT & Happy!

DAY 162
Sleeping in without guilt
Believing in yourself
Friends brave enough to tell you that you messed up
Now It's Your Turn!

1.
2.
3.

DAY 163
Sleeping on freshly laundered sheets
People watching in Manhattan
Not having to over explain
Now It's Your Turn!

1.
2.
3.

DAY 164
Ice skating on frozen ponds
Under-eye beauty marks
Polishing black patent leather Mary Jane's with Vaseline
Now It's Your Turn!

1.
2.
3.

DAY 165
A partner that thinks you are prettier without make-up
Knowing what you want
Saying No!
Now It's Your Turn!

1.
2.
3.

DAY 166

Letting them look - Not being triggered
Late autumn camping trips
Wild turkey footprints on the roof
Now It's Your Turn!

1.

2.

3.

DAY 167

Not needing air conditioning
Carrying a purse that has everything I need
Giving away the clothes that don't fit
Now It's Your Turn!

1.

2.

3.

DAY 168

Finally forgiving yourself
Full length mirrors
64 unbroken crayons
Now It's Your Turn!

1.

2.

3.

This week, I will devote at least 1 hour in reflection on my personal growth journey to FATT & Happy.

NOTES

Key 25

Keeping Up The FATT

When you make a decision to be inspired and uplifted by simple things, you feel happier. This practice is not a magic wand. Challenges don't just disappear. You have to make regular investments in time and energy to get to the root of what's eating at you, and then put in the work to fix it. Making a conscious effort to answer the tough questions is a great start. Looking for three things a day makes a huge difference.

Will you keep doing it?

1. **What discoveries have you made about your life during the FATT & Happy journey?**

2. **What Key impacted you the most?**

3. **What will you do differently as a result of going through this coaching journey?**

4. **What ONE thing makes you feel beautiful? How can you incorporate more of that into your everyday life?**

5. What is one strategy you can use if you are feeling unattractive, having a "bad body" day, "bad hair" day, etc.)?

6. Set a timer for 30 seconds and quickly write down what you are grateful for, as quickly as you can. Don't stop to contemplate. Just make the list. Use additional space in the notes section.

7. Go back through each Key and find your 3 favorite "FATT & Happy Thoughts". Record them below.

8. Throughout this book, I shared some of my personal favorite FATT & Happy discoveries with you. Did anything specifically resonate with you? If so, great! Did you also reserve time each day to Focus Attention & Take Time? List a few of your favorite discoveries here.

GEMS & STRATEGIES

I started my FATT & Happy daily discoveries because I was tired of feeling bad about myself all the time. I had a wonderful faith and worship-centered life. I had a strong marriage. I had healthy, intelligent and well-behaved children. I had a well-paying career. I travelled regularly and enjoyed the perks and benefits of what corporate life had to offer. So much of my life was excellent. And yet so much was lost.

So many times, I missed it, paying more attention to the circumference of my waist and thighs and the stretch marks on my body, than I did to the life my body allowed me to experience. It was a dishonest, unhealthy and embarrassing way to exist. Making the decision to witness my life in micro-mini doses of joyful discoveries started something amazing: Embracing my waistline and finding joy every day, a few moments at a time!

Of course, tough questions and difficult life situations abound. This practice is just scratching the surface. But when you turn the corner you are able to see what could possibly be on the other side. It allows you to see that deeper lasting happiness is actually possible.

What about you? What have you missed that you are now determined to witness? Hopefully this journey has shown you how to confront your truth and create strategies to overcome the little annoyances that trigger negativity so you can release it and let your positivity reign in your brain, in your business and beyond!

Use the categories below to identify and acknowledge what steals your confidence and joy. What strategies can you create when these triggers arise?

<u>**Self-Talk/Negative Thinking**</u>

<u>**Friends/Relationships**</u>

<u>**Habits/Routines**</u>

<u>**Clothes/Personal Image**</u>

<u>**Eating & Food/Body Image**</u>

<u>**Speaking Up**</u>

<u>**Other**</u>

Happily, you also have positive triggers! These make you feel confident, powerful, assertive and beautiful, despite concerns you might have about your body or appearance. Use the categories below to identify and acknowledge what areas bring out the very best in you. What can you do to increase these areas?

Self-Talk/Positive Thinking

Friends/Relationships

Habits/Routines

Clothes/Personal Image

Eating & Food/Body Image

Speaking Up

Other

Additional Resources

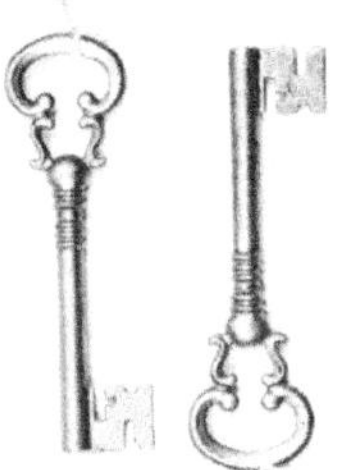

RICE FOR LIFE

The RICE method is often employed when you sprain or strain a muscle or have an injury. It's a quick way of remembering helpful and healthful things to do to aid in your recovery.

- **Rest**
- **Ice**
- **Compression**
- **Elevation**

This works physically because the body needs a variety of actions and modalities to heal. Emotionally we are much the same.

FATT & Happy is a great way to get in mini doses of self-care and rest every single day. When you keep this up, little strains and pains feel better. No doubt throughout this process you have felt less stressed and hopefully a bit happier. But what can you do when you need a little more? How can you get it?

RICE FOR LIFE is a quick method I developed to help my clients remember how to jump out of a negative situation.

Here's how it works:

1. **REST.** When you are under stress, dealing with emotional or physical overwhelm, feeling tapped out, etc., you need self-care. In fact, by the time you have these feelings you are well overdue for self-care. The first and foremost thing you need is rest. A short break. A nap. Quiet. Getting away from others for a little while. Turning off social media. Silencing your phone and email and notifications. Putting on your 'out of office' message. Give yourself permission to rest.

2. **ICE**. Ice slows things down. When you need to take the sting out of a relationship or situation, think about using ice. In other words, slowing down instead of rushing to make a decision. Cooling off before a conversation becomes aggressive. Or taking a moment to allow yourself to feel your feelings instead of eating or drinking them away. Strains come. Slow down before you deal with them and get over the strain faster.

3. **COMPRESSION**. When you are swollen with hurt feelings, confusion, doubt, lack of confidence or clarity, you need compression. Compression keeps the swelling down; it's your tight tribe or trusted friends, accountability partners, coaches, consultants, mentors and advisors. When stress mounts and extra care is needed, you need to be with people who are loyal and like-minded.

4. **ELEVATION**. When you have sustained an injury, you need to put that injured body part in an elevated position. Keeping it at the same level is uncomfortable. You are no different. Even if you need to take a step back in one area or another, a good life is continually seeking the next level. The positive energy of elevation is a powerful curer.

CONSIDER

Where do you need to use this method right now?

38 SELF-CARE IDEAS

1.   Listen to music and dance
2.   Ten minutes of stretching
3.   An at-home face mask
4.   Color in an adult coloring book or doodle freehand
5.   Create a facial from natural ingredients
6.   Fast for clarity
7.   Leave the room and stand anyplace quiet in your home for 5 minutes
8.   Brew a pot of herbal tea from loose leaves and drink slowly
9.   Listen to an inspirational or motivation podcast
10. Pray
11. Go to a nearby park and listen to or watch nature
12. Wake before anyone else and spend a few moments in contemplation
13. Focus Attention & Take Time with a friend
14. Unplug for a day
15. Practice an instrument
16. Wear an outfit you love, even if you have nowhere special to go
17. Say No
18. Sit in a rocking chair and re-read a favorite book
19. Daydream
20. Set an alarm to watch the next sunrise or sunset
21. Wear a new lipstick
22. Write a list of FATT & Happy moments
23. Go for a drive without a destination
24. Diffuse your favorite essential oil throughout your home
25. Take a bubble bath with scented salts and bath bombs
26. Go outside for a short walk
27. Visit a local museum or art gallery
28. Eat a small decadent treat
29. Simplify your schedule
30. Eat lunch for 20 minutes
31. Write down a gratitude list
32. Sit in a coffee shop and watch passersby
33. Paint your nails
34. Soak your feet
35. Rub essential oil into your hands or the soles of your feet – or both
36. Five minutes of measured breathing
37. Leisurely leaf through a printed magazine
38. Go to bed early

25 STRATEGIES FOR BETTER BODYCON

1. Make a list of your gifts (Key 23)

2. Give extra attention to your hair and wear makeup (Key 7)

3. Stay away from energy draining people for 24-48 hours (Key 6)

4. Go for a power walk, get moving (Key 8)

5. Wear a fierce handbag and if you can, wear heels (Key 7)

6. Pick an outfit that you have received compliments on in the past (Key 5)

7. Protect your bandwidth (Key 18)

8. Do something for someone else, extra kindness goes a long way (Key 2)

9. Wear all black with a pop of color or animal print (Key 5)

10. Don't spend time looking for proof that you're not good enough (Key 15)

11. Challenge yourself to counter every negative thought about yourself with at least 2 positive ones (Key 19)

12. Wear a body shaper or good foundation garment (Key 5)

13. Review who you have been associating with lately (Key 6, Key 13)

14. Counter shame with love (Key 21)

15. Be gentle and patient with yourself (Key 19)

16. Think of all the wonderful things your body does for you (Key 4)

17. Be grateful; your worst day is the best for someone else (Key 1)

18. Know your "cute" uniform and wear it (Key 5)

19. Observe something beautiful in nature (Key 1)

20. Stall making big decisions (Key 18)

21. Practice self-care (Key 24)

22. Eat a light, but well-prepared meal (Key 21)

23. Clean your bedroom, your car, or a corner of your desk (Key 6)

24. Dress like you love it anyway (Key 10)

25. Ask yourself: Is this actually a physical issue? (Key 11)

25 INTENTIONS TO LIVE BY

1. This week, I will pay attention to my self-talk and correct self-defeating language.
2. This week, I will give myself permission to feel my feelings, instead of stuffing them down.
3. This week, I will release one painful memory that no longer serves me.
4. Each day this week, I will give a compliment to someone I encounter.
5. This week, I will make a list of my growth and accomplishments from the last 30 days.
6. This week, I will do something decadent for myself and my best friend.
7. This week, I will call or send a card to someone who needs it and tell them about their specialness.
8. This week, I will be 100% honest *and* straight-forward during a difficult conversation at work or home.
9. This week, I will increase my movement and I will admire something about my physical appearance during the process.
10. This week, I will get one extra hour of sleep each night.
11. This week, I will ask for help in 1-2 areas where I have needed it the most.
12. This week, I will work hard to substitute negative thoughts with neutral ones.
13. This week, I will purge 3 items from my closet that no longer fit, I no longer wear, or that bring unwelcome thoughts to my mind.
14. This week, I will clean up one area in my home or office.
15. Starting this week, I will let go of comparing myself to others.
16. This week, I will practice eating eat only when I am hungry for at least 2 days. I will feed my mind generously on positivity every day.
17. This week, I will recognize and celebrate my inner strength.
18. This week I will stare into the mirror and repeat: "I Am Beautiful. I Am Enough."
19. This week, I will speak up respectfully at work. I will use my voice. I will share my ideas.
20. This week, I will practice self-care by declining what I know will stretch me beyond what I can healthily do.
21. This week, I will forgive myself for not moving on sooner.
22. This week, I will take a stand against body, weight and food shaming.
23. This week, I will encourage someone who needs it by calling, sending a text, writing a card, or stopping by their home.
24. This week, I will give my most important relationship more of the real me.
25. This week, I will devote at least 1 hour in reflection on my personal growth journey to FATT & Happy.

FINAL KEY THOUGHTS FROM CHATONE

- *See your unique gifts as something special set aside just for you. The benefits, credibility and opportunities you can receive from appropriately using them can change your life.*

- *Speak up when you know you should. Silence doesn't serve.*

- *Other people can't read your mind. Before you say "yes", consider your reasons why, and understand to what you are saying "no", as a result.*

- *Your physical body whispers to you and tells you when something isn't right. Learn to listen to what it is saying through how you physically feel. One visceral response goes a long way.*

- *Despite popular belief, you have the right to take up space. Today's average woman is bigger than in years past. A curvy size 16-18 is as beautiful and worthy as a woman half her size and vice-versa. Allow this to make you feel free and beautiful regardless of your size.*

- *If a relationship or situation is completely draining your energy, consider reducing it or eliminating it altogether, if possible.*

- *Every 30 days list your growth and accomplishments. Never miss an opportunity to acknowledge how far you've come, and where you can still go.*

- *Growth happens when you are accountable.*

- *Celebrate who you are right now. Being in the present moment is not looking at the past or the future. Getting rid of the old clothes in your closet that no longer represent who you are or no longer fit, is a way to celebrate who you are today!*

- *Focus Attention and Take Time every day. Embrace the whole you and add a little dose of joy to every single day.*

- **Be FATT & Happy**

*"Be Authentic.
Be Brilliant.
Be the Catalyst."*

Chatone Morrison

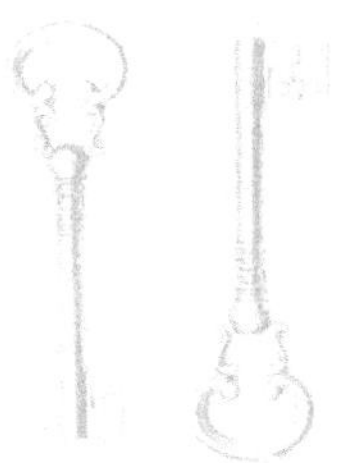

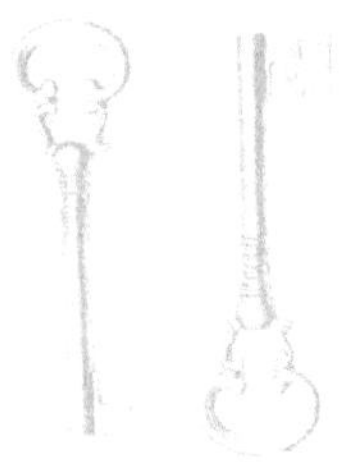

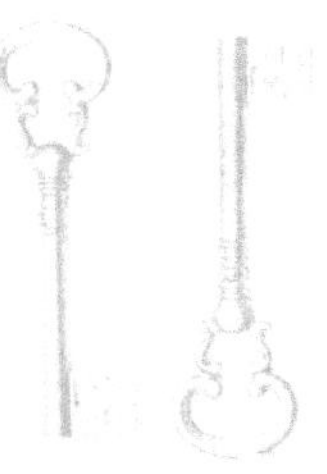

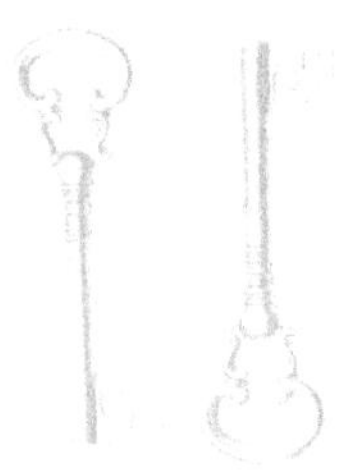

REFERENCES

- *You are invited to join Chatone in her social media community on Instagram: @fattandhappylife*

- *If you are a coach or counselor interested in using this book to lead a program or masterclass series, email **admin@chatonemorrison.com** to learn how to leverage this tool for your clients.*

- *To learn more about the services offered by Shaye Cunningham, Personal Stylist & Coach, visit: **https://www.facebook.com/slaybyshaye***

SUGGESTED READING

- *I Thought It Was Just Me (But It Isn't) – Author, Brene Brown*

- *When Food Is Love – Author, Geneen Roth*

- *Appetites – Author, Geneen Roth*

- *Codependent No More – Melody Beattie*

- *Fierce Conversations – Susan Scott*

*Would you like to bring Chatone Morrison to your organization for a speaking engagement, training, team meeting, or special event? Send your query to **admin@chatonemorrison.com** for topics and scheduling availability.*

ABOUT THE AUTHOR

Chatone Morrison is trademarked as the Princess of Positivity® and is the owner of Chatone Morrison Consulting. She is a Content Strategist & Confidence Coach for women, a lifelong poet, and an avid online live broadcaster. If you meet her, she will probably tell you: "Frankly, my dear, you ARE the content!"

Chatone is the founder of the *Confident Content Cafe*™ and the *Confidence Catalyst Academy*™, online writing and creativity communities. She teaches inspiration, motivation and confidence through virtual programs and services, in person workshops, and by working individually with women business owners. Since 2016, Chatone has hosted, *The Sunday Corner*™, a weekly videocast, to help women rejuvenate and refresh before a new week begins.

Passionately, she helps lady entrepreneurs get their confident content written, so they can stop all the stress, and get back to what's most important. Work with her and start embracing her mantra: "Release your negativity and let positivity reign in your brain and in your business."

FATT & Happily, Chatone shares time between Maryland and Florida with her husband Mark and their two children.

For more information on Chatone Morrison Consulting, follow on Facebook:
@chatonemorrisonconsulting or visit the website at chatonemorrison.com.

For additional copies of this book, to purchase in bulk, or to purchase for a non-profit organization, please send an email to admin@chatonemorrison.com.

Made in the USA
Middletown, DE
30 September 2021

48770088R00130